CW00676404

THE ADVENTURES OF
AN ARTISAN HUNTER

THE ADVENTURES
OF AN
ARTISAN HUNTER

David Brian Plummer

Illustrated by Martin Knowelden

COCH-Y-BONDDU BOOKS

First published by The Boydell Press 1979
Reprinted by Coch-y-Bonddu Books 2000
© 1979 David Brian Plummer

ISBN 0 9533648 6 0

To John Winch, M.A.
Thanks for a life-time's friendship.

Published & distributed by
COCH-Y-BONDDU BOOKS
MACHYNLLETH, POWYS, SY20 8DJ
Tel 01654 702837   Fax 01654 702857

CONTENTS

Introduction   7

1. Birds of a Feather?   11

2. Grit and Steel   25

3. The Bird-catchers   41

4. Well, Don't Knock It Till You Try It   55

5. San   69

6. First Hawk   89

7. Climber   99

8. Kitchen Hawk   113

To John Eden – a *rara avis* – an interesting teacher

Introduction

It was only a week before I sat down to write this that I met my old chemistry teacher. School teachers always seem old to children, but he had aged considerably in the twenty-five years since I last saw him. He was an interesting, intelligent teacher, an endangered species twenty-five years ago, and now a decided *rara avis*, so I could not resist rushing across the road to talk to him. Would he remember me after all those years that would have resounded with the clatter of noisy kids' feet? What academic achievement of mine would spring to mind at the moment of recognition, what relic of my scholastic prowess would he remember? I strode up to him. 'Remember me, Mr Palmer sir?' (The sir, slipped out so easily – I've always been naturally subservient, and two years after National Service I was still saluting commissionaires!) Old Palmer looked up at me; the years flashing by behind his rheumy eyes like a chronometrical ticker tape. 'Plummer? Ye-e-e-s, I remember you – you used to sell hedgehogs to the children of the school.'

> O mighty Caesar! dost thou lie so low?
> Are all my conquests, glories, triumphs, spoils
> Sunk to this little measure?

I suppose I've always been regarded as some sort of oddball ever since I was a child, and a South Welsh mining valley is no place for an eccentric, albeit a juvenile eccentric. To the casual observer, every mining valley is seemingly identical – eroded by ice, ruined by man, invigorated by breweries and sublimated by the eternal gloom of the chapels and Welsh publess Sundays. The poet Swinburne must have known all about my valley when he wrote, 'Thou hast triumphed, O pale Galilean; the world has grown grey from thy breath.' Sunday, silent as the grave with the gloom broken only by the sound of trotting feet, when 'holier than thous' trotted up the hill to Bethel chapel. Truly the portals of the Pearly Gates will only open to the sound of trotting, Welsh Sundays, the swish of fox tippets, the clatter of 'sensible' heels and an attitude of mind that killed off more Christians than any lion in the Circus Maximus.

Not all the village was under the black, gloomy shadow of the chapel. Hard districts beget incredible characters. Let no one who has never seen such a place imagine that it is a sterile substrata nourishing colourless characters. Welsh humour is sharp, though to the uninitiated its edges are dulled somewhat by the sing-songy voices of the natives. My father, when he could be persuaded to put down his well-thumbed copy of Karl Marx, or if the *Daily Worker* had not arrived (for not all newspaper strikes are communist inspired), had a dazzling wit and an inquiring mind, though his only claim to fame was that he had been forcibly ejected from Noddfa Spiritualist chapel for asking if he could speak to the spirit of Jesus Christ. An inquiring mind is not always good for you, I was once told by a teacher when I had asked exactly what Kubla Khan kept in his stately pleasure dome.

Shakespeare wrote most of his work in London. If he had attempted to write the 'Seven Ages of Man' passage from *As You Like It* in a South Welsh coalfield, it would have read as follows. Stage one: the schoolboy struggling desperately not to attend a school ruled tyrannically by untrained matrons whose only qualification for teaching was that they could hiss spittle into the faces of terrified infants as they badgered them into reading. On to grammar school for stage two, where bland intellectuals, intolerably boring, tried to drum some little knowledge into unretentive heads and P.E. staff lectured us on the error of our unhealthy ways, standing straight-backed, their spinal columns terminating in very empty craniums. Stage three: a quick and often unfulfilled snatch at puberty, then the inevitable all-consuming soul-destroying pub, in which my father spent a good two thirds of his waking life, partly to discuss politics and partly to escape my mother's wicked harridan tongue. Next, when the magic of under-age drinking had lost some of its magnetic charm, a few years of pigeon flying, of rattling tins of corn while gazing southwards with anxious expression. Then a return to the pubs, or working men's clubs as some of them masqueraded in order to escape the Sunday drinking laws.

By fifty, the Welsh miner of my youth was a broken man. His mind underdeveloped, though often acute, his stomach corroded by the awful scrumpy or rough cider – made, I believe, from one part apple juice, four parts cleaning fluid – and his lungs blitzed by silicosis, his back bent through hewing coal in confined spaces. Sans teeth, sans hair, sans lungs, sans spirit, sans all. By the age of twelve I knew I was suffering from a very bad case of homesickness, for I was thoroughly sick of home and resolved to leave.

1 *Birds of a Feather?*

Somewhere in the maze of lanes between Cowbridge and Porthcawl lives the last descendant of the race that spawned the Cyclops, Fee Fi Fo Fum, Sawney Bean, the notorious man-eater of Galloway: a latter-day demon Asmodeus. Scientists bluff us by telling us these things are merely race memories. I alone know the truth, but as usual I have run ahead of my tale.

I must have been about twelve at the time, and playing truant fairly regularly. The reason for my failure or reluctance to attend school was the physics teacher, who cherished the unique educational theory that I could be best taught Ohm's Law, etcetera, by having my head pounded against the brickwork of the physics-lab wall. Oddly enough I did not share his enthusiasm for such methods, and often emerged from his physics lesson more badly bruised than after I had fought six rounds with Terry Downes's sparring partner. He seemed literally baffled as to why I did not enjoy the kicking and beating and was amazed when I played truant from his lessons. So totally did he kill my enthusiasm for his subject that a fuse has only to blow to find me frantically phoning an electrician friend rather than attempt the repair myself.

At first I began by hiding in the lavatories, a place beloved and well frequented by truants, but a death trap, for any teacher worth his salt will first check the toilets before beginning a lesson. So I resolved not to attend school on the days when physics was being taught to my class. Tuesdays and Thursdays I would slip my black mongrel, wave good-bye to Mam, retrace my steps, pick up the dog and spend the day ratting or hunting hedgehogs which abounded on the bracken of the hillsides. Wednesdays and Fridays, at 9 a.m., would find me outside the head's office for my thrashing. So regular were my habits that Kellogg's might well

11

have used me as an advert for All-Bran. I never once thought of retaliating against this physics-lab tyrant – it just wasn't that sort of school, and anyway, he was bigger than I was. Looking back on those unhappy years spent dodging and ducking blows and learning, I am amazed that my headmaster did not follow up the reason why I failed to attend school on those particular days, but he probably found it easier to cane. 'When in doubt – thrash' was a dictum adopted by most teachers during my youth.

I took to walking to the lower end of the valley – a village called Brynmenyn – 'the hill with a mill' in English, a place some six miles distant from my home and until then a location unspoilt by the mining that had scarred the rest of the valley. Here rabbits could be found eking out a somewhat sparse existence on the edges of the hills, and grass snakes drawn by the warmth of the Tondu coke ovens curled like silvery green bands round the roots of alders. The river here was relatively clean, for the detritus of the coal washeries had been dropped up-stream, and where the rivers Ogmore and Garw joined, sea trout, or *sewen* as the Welsh called them, as much at home in fresh as in salt water, lay fanning their silvery bodies in the deep pools out of reach of hands and sticks. It was a far cry from any physics lab where I would be ducking punches and learning like some academic Harry Greb. Such pleasantries were well worth the resulting thrashings from both parents and headmaster. Brynmenyn holds a lot of magic for me, for not only was it the district where I could indulge in all my wilder interests, but it was a place where I was to meet my chubby *alter ego*, the neighbouring town of Maesteg's equivalent of me, but, unlike me, one of the most quick-witted, lightning-tongued people I have ever met.

I had skipped school for my usual Tuesday/Thursday reasons and walked through the muddy woodlands of Pandy to Brynmenyn. On the hillside my black mongrel was casting among the gorse bushes that made the hillside a patchwork of green and yellow the whole year round, for the saying that kissing's not in season when the gorse is not in bloom is a true one. He was working like a demon, tail bespeaking his remote setter ancestry, head down to drink in the delicious scent of ground game. He stopped and lifted his paw, his tail as straight as a field-trial pointer. A rabbit shot out of the gorse and raced up the hill. My mongrel yelped slightly and gave chase, but he was a heavy dog and had no chance of catching it. I watched the rabbit turn at the top of the slope and saw a rough-coated lurcher, scruffy but useful, snap up the rabbit with the speed of a conjurer fielding a ball out of the air. The dog returned the rabbit to his owner, a short fat boy about my own age, but still wearing short trousers. He was so exactly like Lewis Carroll's Tweedledum that I waited a moment for his brother to come into view, but my new-found companion was indeed a one-off job – I doubt if Maesteg could have coped with two of his ilk.

There is a saying that looks often belie the personality of a man, and this was a case in point. My little fat friend was just over a year older than I was, and in addition to being highly articulate (I was still stammering badly), he had a dazzlingly quick mind. His mother, who ruled the family with a rod of iron, insisted that Derek should stay ever young by decreeing that he should wear short trousers (if she could have kept him a child forever by hormone injections I believe she would have done so). He, too, was a renegade, desperately avoiding English literature, which was taught by a master who, having probably trained at a similar establishment to my physics teacher, was convinced that *David Copperfield* went down best after a karate chop or so to the throat. Derek couldn't take it and simply refused to attend school, and so together we must have constituted a unique hunting combination. Come to think of it, he must have made me look very foolish – me with my fearful stutter, and him with an eloquence second to none. Story has it his mother could claim descent from Twm Sion Cati, the legendary Welsh hero, a none too judicious blend of Robin Hood and Max Boyce; but about one in four Welshmen lay claim to such descent. Funnily enough, when I look back to this youthful vagabond, his mother's story just could be correct for her son had all the attributes of the Cardiganshire folk hero. For the next three years we became great friends, and in spite of the eight miles that separated our homes, we hunted together regularly.

Derek was a born leader of men, and had a gang of somewhat younger acolytes in attendance wherever he went – eager to follow and ape this little fat boy whose appearance must have seemed comical, even to them. But in spite of his quaint shape and the fact that his foolish and doting mother, clucking like an old hen, would rush out on to the street to comb his hair in public, he had the same dynamism and charisma that must have characterized Napoleon at the Battle of Marengo. He would insist on absolute devotion from his acolytes, and was for ever devising absurdly dangerous initiation tests to try their courage – tests which involved him hurling their caps over the high stone wall of the garden that housed one of Maesteg's first Alsatians, and when the boys retrieved the cap and tried to scale back over the wall, he would stamp on their hands. Two were badly mauled as a result of these antics, but still followed him, devoted to the last. I imagine Lycurgus, who drew up the very harsh laws that governed Sparta, must have been a similar type of dynamic kink. Derek's attempt to initiate me into his gang ended up in a severe fight between us, vicious as only adolescent battles can be.

My test had been to go into the local Working Men's Institute and shout, 'Will Evans is a bastard!' at one of the older men in the reading room. Will, then well into his fifties, had a fearsome reputation. He was a noted street fighter in his youth, and legend had it that in one of the inter-valley battles that had been all too common during the Depression, he had bitten the nose off an opponent as they battled it out on the tops of the hills. Perhaps the story had been made up or grew with time, but Will had been one of the most feared men in the village. In spite of his reputation for ferocity, middle age had made him overweight and so the task of rushing up the stairs, shouting my party piece and racing out through the front doors was not as formidable as it appeared – or so I thought!

I walked in through the back entrance, up the stairs to where Will sat reading the newspaper. 'Will Evans is-s-s-s-s . . .' and words failed me as my stuttering returned. He got the gist of it, though, and was after me in a trice. I raced down the stairs to the front doors, but was unable to open them as Derek was holding the handles on the other side. Will gave me a terrific cuffing before I managed to escape his fury, made worse by Derek shouting through the letter box, 'Bite his nose off, Will.' I managed to get away at the back, however, nostrils intact, and rushed around to the front to fight Derek who, aware of my anger, was desperately waddling for home. If one wants further proof of his charisma – well, I still followed him even after that encounter.

I was fairly certain his strange sense of humour would be the death of him, for his sense of daring bordered on the suicidal. His glandular disorder would have prevented escape even when pursued by a Galapagos turtle, but he would still attempt the most outrageous deeds – the sort of lad who commits *hara-kiri* just for the hell of it, or gets someone else to do it for him! A case springs instantly to mind. He had found an old lorry inner tube and had set to work organizing his band to cut twigs to make catapults, the best of which he confiscated as his kingly right – if he had demanded the right of *prima nocte* with their intended wives I believe they would have complied. Fat and funny as he looked, he was deadly with this piece of rustic artillery. I was singularly inept and made to look all the more foolish by my friend's ease and accuracy with the weapon. On reflection, Derek was bad for me in every way.

To get missiles for his catapults proved quite a task, and together with other luckless slaves I dug in the pit-waste piles of the near-by colliery for the ironstone nodules, tiny red blobs of haematite that enclosed a brazen pyrites core. They were accurate projectiles, flew true and fast, but lacked size. Eventually it was our lord and master who solved the problem. We were walking along the railway track, searching for slowworms under the flat stones of the embankment, or trying to catch adders as they lay sunning themselves, striped and deadly, on the warm stones of the dry bank. Out of the blue he said, 'My Dad has a huge spanner!' I had no doubt of the truth of this statement for his father was a fitter at the local pit, but felt a little mystified as to what the state- ment had to do with present happenings. Next day he returned with a giant wrench carried by acolytes. Carefully he unscrewed some of the nuts that held the railway track to the fishplates, taking two or three nuts every few hundred yards. I was aghast and had visions of the late-night Saturday train, called for some strange reason 'the Raglan', carrying drunken revellers from Bridgend (my father among them), derailed and spewing debris and dead drunks all over the track. It never happened. Perhaps the railway staff checked that area of the line regularly, or maybe fishplates don't actually hold the track in place. I don't really know – and Derek, who probably did know, didn't care.

These nuts were deadly pieces of equipment, and being of a fairly regular shape they flew absolutely true. To test his missiles he visited his aunt's house, knowing she would be working that day at the local lunatic asylum called Angelton. ('They turn the lunatics loose at night, to eat frogs and things,' Derek had told the younger members of the gang, as if disclosing that he had some secret knowledge of a new psychiatric cure.) After a quick look round to make sure there were no witnesses, he fired the fishplate nut at the door of his aunt's house. It flew fast and true, smashing a highly polished panel of the door to pieces before he ran off. 'Terrible vandalism in the district,' his aunt said to his mother that night, and Tweedledum, having his hair combed by Mummy, merely nodded his head and smiled.

Armed with such lethal bolts, there was now no stopping our hero, and nothing was safe. Crows, jackdaws, domestic pigeons foolish enough to perch away from the loft, all bit the dust to be retrieved to hand by his adoring followers, more like spaniels than gang members. Cats became suddenly scarce in the district, and it was rumoured that a poisoner was at work (it was common practice for pigeon flyers to poison cats who came too near their lofts). Derek's stubby little arms were amazingly powerful, and little lived after a collision with a flying fishplate nut. In the light of the damage done to his aunt's door, I am frankly surprised that the army has never patented this type of weapon.

We were wandering around the outskirts of Bridgend. 'Gutless, gutless', he was chanting to chide me. He was going through his daily, 'Anything you can do I can do better,' made all the more infuriating because he could. 'Gutless' was his worst insult, meaning lack of courage. 'Gutless, gutless,' he cried, leaping up and down in an insane parody of a dance. I can't remember why he was chiding me – perhaps I had refused to fight a rugby-playing bully, or maybe refused to leap off Brynmenyn bridge into the path of an oncoming train – anyway, it is of no importance. We were now deep inside a private game estate, well set out with lakes and the compulsory rhododendron bushes, and he was perhaps feeling just a little niggly because he had shot a lovely Amherst pheasant that I had failed to retrieve from a thicket for him.

'Mouth, that's all you are,' I stammered, taking a full ten minutes to eject my insult, that had lost something of its edge in the translation. A small troop of Chinese geese, elegant with black stripe from bill to shoulder, strolled innocently into the road and walked calmly down the lane.

'Show you, show you,' he hissed and let fly a nut. The gander dropped instantly, flapping loudly, the top of its cranium completely blown off.

I had started to run at the instant of collision, but he blandly waved me back. He hid his catapult and heavy pouch of ammunition under a hedge and walked towards the gander that had now ceased its struggles. He picked up the limp bird and walked towards the estate house. 'Oh, my God,' I thought, 'he's gone barmy,' and stood ready to make yet another run for it. I watched him walk up the short drive from my hiding place near the gate. This estate was owned by a Major Bagott or Bagnell – I'm not sure which – and Derek, wearing his ever-present ridiculous school cap, dusted down his jacket and knocked at the door.

'Found your goose, Major Bagott/Bagnell, some rotten thing has shot it,' said Derek looking sorrowful.

'Oh, *darrw* [Welsh expression denoting sorrow or concern], it's the gander, too – I'll never replace him,' said the moustachioed, straight-backed little man, eyeing the fishy-eyed cadaver rapidly cooling in Derek's arms. 'Glad to see there's still some concern for animals left in the younger generation though,' he said, glumly reaching into his pocket for a ten-shilling note, which he gave to Derek, who tried, but not too hard, to refuse it. As he took the money he touched his cap, and then walked sadly back towards me with such conviction that I felt like whistling 'The Dead March'. The door closed and we were in the lane again.

'Gutless, gutless,' he cried, letting fly another volley at the feeding geese.

If Tweedledum was a puzzle, so was his lurcher Sion (his mother had named it after her illustrious ancestor). Sion was a rough-coated slinky-bodied dog of mixed and unknown ancestry. ('Sired the greatest Waterloo Cup dog ever,' Derek told everybody.) At the age of eleven, Derek had come down with some unusual glandular disease (hence the podge), and darling Mummy, still combing his hair, had thought her loved one was about to die. Sensing that he would not be denied his last requests, Derek had asked for outlandish things. Ferrets, a lurcher, an airgun, all the things that Mummy would have instantly labelled as 'common' and have refused him. Like the treacherous little rogue he was, immediately he acquired these things he promptly began to recover, though relapses tended to be common when anything he wanted was denied him. So Mummy had sent Daddy around the country into the lairs of the seedy and unwholesome (a far cry from the chapels) to procure a lurcher puppy for her dying son,

17

preferably a long-haired lurcher, for had said loving son died, she would at least have had something still to comb. Daddy slavishly searched the countryside to procure a lurcher puppy for the ailing child. It would have been quite fascinating to watch ultra-respectable Daddy negotiating with the typical rascals who bred lurchers in the post-war days, but eventually he turned up with a scrawny, shaggy puppy.

Sion had an obviously very mixed ancestry. His silky topknot denoted Bedlington, his sagacity and cunning suggested collie, and the rest – well, mostly greyhound with the inevitable dash of Heinz (the same type is usually sold today as deerhound/greyhound). Whatever the mix, the brew was a potent one. Sion was one hell of a dog, even by adult standards, and to a child he was something out of another world. Dad had picked him up near Spalding, a district famed for its hares and a testing ground second to none for a lurcher. Not only was he bred properly, but he had plenty of practice and an abundance of good, though youthful, training. Sportsmen, I bid you beware, a child and a well-bred lurcher are a fearful combination to beat. Not only is a child unhampered by marital commitments and job, but he is also able to develop a very fine link with an animal of a kind that few adults, least of all the professional trainer, could ever dream of. Furthermore, not only was my fat friend 'good' with dogs, he had that rare quality called intelligence – sadly, a bit of a novelty in hunters today.

Sion was an incredible dog, more suited to a gipsy camp than a 'nice to be nice' chapel house (but come to think of it, so was Derek). I have many times seen the animal crawl under a five-bar gate and creep belly to earth (like a stalking cat) towards a flock of feeding pigeons (wild or homers, Derek wasn't that fussy), and strike madly at them, chopping this way and that; but by the time the flock had risen, he would have laid low two or more. There was precious little game in the valleys, for the hills had been shorn of sheltering trees by the early dwellers, but in a 'fat' game country Sion would really have made a name for himself, and probably have gone on to become a lurcher legend. He was equally as good as my own mongrel at rat killing, and at the sport of rabbiting – a game that requires a short, sharp dash after the disappearing prey – he was hard to beat. Time maybe dims the memory, and this was twenty-seven years ago, but in the way of lurchers at least

I have myself owned nothing to beat Sion. The staple quarry of the lurcher, however, is the hare, and there were few enough hares in our valley.

I suppose the following disaster was of my own doing, but I will apportion the blame equally between myself and Derek. He was as much to blame for his treachery as I was for my stupidity. I had gone to Cardiff on a school trip to see the museum, where stuffed birds, looking nothing like their live counterparts, gazed out at the bored crowds with just a hint of cynicism and signs like, 'This bird was shot by the Marquis of ——. It is now an extinct species,' bespeaking man's stupidity, festooned the showcases. It was a typical school trip: a lot of eating, a smatter of a dirty song rapidly hushed by an embarrassed junior member of staff, a brief omnibus love affair or so, and home again with vomiting as compulsory extra. I was far too impoverished to be able to afford sweets, and stuttered so badly that most girls found me amusingly quaint or pitied me, so I spent my time gazing out of the windows at the changing countryside. Starting at Pontycymer, through to Bridgend, where story had it that the population was so wealthy that their houses sported bathrooms, and then, twelve miles from home, to Cowbridge, a snooty little village where somehow the sing-song Welsh accent of the valleys had not been acquired. We had just pulled out of Cowbridge when I saw him.

Nothing is more fascinating than the sight of one's first live hare, unless, of course, it be the sight of one's lurcher returning with one's first dead one. He stood upright in the still dewy grass, his black-tipped ears held erect as if expecting danger and his coat shiny with the health and vitality only obtainable through fat pastures and freedom. 'Jesus Christ,' I hissed, 'he's as big as a dog'; and he scampered off in the effortless, unhurried manner that is so deceptive. My day in the museum passed slowly, for its long-dead menagerie and fossilized plants and people held little magic for me. I was itching to be home to tell Derek of my find and to plan how and when to take our hare.

In the event, he seemed oddly unenthusiastic about the whole business when I blurted out my story. In spite of his bombastic attitude, he never once ridiculed my stammer and waited rather impatiently for the end of my tale. 'O.K., we'll take him Tuesday' (physics and English). Oh, the optimism of youth, to casually brush aside one of nature's masterpieces with a gesture of the

19

hand. It was to be weeks before we eventually managed to catch one.

I lay awake that Monday night, my mind filled with safari-type visions of Derek walking dog on leash and me staggering under the weight of a dozen hares, but it was not to be. Reader, I beg you mistrust those adverts in *Exchange and Mart* that claim, 'This dog will take four out of four hares.' Such dogs are seldom born and never sold. A hare has a wondrous burst of speed and an ability to stop in full flight by turning in its own length, rather like a startled politician, I've always thought. Furthermore, they know the ground on which they live, every tussock of grass, every weakness in a hedge, every gap under a gate, and they use them to advantage when pressed. The very fact that a hare, unlike a rabbit, has no hole in which to hide makes the creature exceedingly alert, for it has no place to run when danger threatens. Furthermore, its running muscles – that is, the muscles concerned with propulsion – occupy a third of its body weight, but marvel of marvels, dissection of a dead hare reveals a heart as large as a baby's fist. The hare is truly one of the masterpieces of the Almighty's workshop, and to take one is a really killing task for the inexperienced dog.

To cut a long story short, we ran two hares that day, both of which Sion looked like taking, and both of which escaped at the end of the chase. We returned home disconsolate. The quality that separates coursing men from coursing boys is that men learn to appreciate the chase for itself, whereas a child has to have a kill to show for its troubles. The chases were both pieces of athleticism, but as Sion had failed to connect, well – we regarded the day as a failure. The fact that Sion snapped a moorhen out of the air as we trudged our way through the forbidden grounds of the mental hospital (Derek even too miserable to make jokes about the misfortunes of the inmates) did little to dispel the gloom.

Holidays! And every day spent poaching the Cowbridge farms, sometimes ignored by the farmers, but more often than not driven off with oaths and curses. How wonderfully fit I must have been in those days. Cowbridge was a full twelve miles from home, and we would walk maybe fifty miles on a good day, living on berries and spring water. I was as thin as a lath to begin with, and very fit, but Tweedledum, fat and puffing as he always was, kept up with me every step of the way. Considering the number of hares we must have run, it was inevitable that sooner or later we would catch one, and the day we did was a red-letter day in my life. The sight of a running dog striking repeatedly at a bobbing, ducking, weaving hare, and suddenly coming up with it in its mouth, is a sight that has delighted poets and lovers of the chase for centuries. We raced for home, our feet barely touching the ground and avoiding the main roads where the sight of our illegally taken hare might cause concern. First, we went to Maesteg, to Derek's house, where hair-combing Mummy displayed a mixture of pride and chapel-bred concern for her son. Then we went to my own home eight miles over the hills, but my mother and father, engaged in one of their perpetual domestic quarrels, scarcely listened to my stuttered version of our hunt. On reflection, how limited the outlook of my parents was, and how petty-minded their views seem to me now.

The hare was the first of several we took that summer, and sooner or later the junior poacher starts taking enormous risks to get a run, and sooner or later he gets caught. We had probably run all the hares off the farms around Cowbridge – they were never very numerous – and we were now poaching the land along the lanes between Cowbridge and Porthcawl. My black mongrel, enthusiastic but slow, had put up a hare and both dogs had gone off in pursuit. Sion soon outstripped my dog and was soon running the hare solo. There is something mesmerizing about the contest between dog and hare, a quality that blots out all other cares but, more dangerous still, anaesthetizes one's sense of caution. It was therefore only after a few minutes that I realized I was being watched. I dived for cover behind a large bramble patch on the edge of the field, leaving Derek fat and helpless. Helpless? Well, I reckoned without his quick wits and alarming lack of loyalty. A gaunt, jaundiced man, face furious, strode into the field. Tweedledum raced over towards him.

'If you're looking for the poacher, sir, he's behind the bush, sir.' (Derek always threw in an extra 'sir' for good measure, particularly when frightened.) 'There's his dog, sir' – pointing at *his* lurcher. (Another 'sir', he really must have been frightened.)

The man was on me in a trice, and seizing me by the arm, he half-lifted, half-dragged me past the little fat school-uniformed boy with a cap – who looked nothing like a poacher. I was dragged up the land towards his cottage. 'He's going to fetch the police,' I thought, panic-stricken, but as we neared his house, a picture postcard country cottage with carefully kept garden, I had a sudden horrid vision of a Hansel and Gretel ending to the story, with me being cooked in an oven and my little Judas friend probably invited in to tea. Not a word was spoken as he opened the door and thrust me inside the house. His tasteful cottage held a bland and tasteful wife who, silent as he was, handed him a cane. In absolute silence, he belaboured me savagely for a full ten minutes, leaving me black and blue, my body covered in red weals and slash marks. When he was damned-nigh exhausted, he opened the door and literally threw me out, clicking the catch behind me. Derek was totally unabashed about his lack of loyalty, and acting as though nothing untoward had happened, he walked home with me without so much as an apology.

Betrayal was just a way of life to Derek, and it came as second nature to him. As we limped into puberty together he brought a great deal of trouble my way. Once when we wandered into the dockland world of Cardiff, known to the outside world as Tiger Bay, we were suddenly jumped by a gang of black youths. 'What yer doing here?' – how strange to hear a Welsh accent coming from a black face. 'We are Gods; bow down and worship us,' said Derek quietly. They gave him a long, hard look, decided he was nuts and treated me to a savage beating. Another time, talking to a gang of Teddy-boys complete with drainpipe trousers, girl friend and other regalia of the age, 'If you don't leave her alone, my friend says he will come over and smash your faces,' he said challengingly. They dragged me outside. I was totally unable to protest my innocence because of my stammer, made ten times worse by fear. 'Just asked her out,' said Tweedledum chirpily a moment after my torturers had left me for dead across the frozen-drinks containers at the rear of the dance hall.

Well, shortly after my sixteenth birthday I had a tremendous row with my father and left home for good. I never saw my parents again. I wrote to Derek several times from Poland, Germany and even Egypt, but I suspect that Mummy, fearing Tweedledum would join me, intercepted my letters. Apparently she needn't have worried. Time passed and I was well into my thirties before I saw Derek again.

I had gone to Cheltenham to mate my greyhound bitch to a particularly good lurcher dog, a blue, rough-coated animal, and stayed to do a spot of coursing with my greyhound and a friend's lurcher. Evening found me tired and muddy, lying on the verge opposite a small pub waiting for my current girl friend to pick me up. A coach pulled up, full of respectable old ladies off on a respectable old outing. A portly vicar, podgy and sweating under his dog collar, helped them off the bus. There was something oddly familiar about his chubby hind-quarters, but it was a full five minutes before I recognized who it was.

'Good God, Derek!' I uttered.

He turned. 'Brian,' he said, suddenly beaming. He beckoned the old ladies towards the conveniences and we began to talk. It took me five seconds flat to realize we were now worlds apart. His accent had gone and the sight of my muddy clothes brought a pained look to his face.

'What happened to the stammer?' he said, half embarrassed, after we had exchanged a few neutral pleasantries.

'Left it in some woman's bedroom,' I answered, the reply all the more ludicrous for being true.

'Oh,' he said, desperately thinking of something to say. 'Nice dogs,' he murmured.

'Like to see a run?' I asked, watching his face carefully.

'Er, er, not just now,' he said, looking decidedly uneasy.

'Gutless, gutless,' I whispered, lapsing so easily into the old childhood vernacular.

'I'll give you a ring,' he shouted a little sheepishly, helping the old ladies back on the coach.

He never did, of course.

2 *Grit and Steel*

I think I must have been about thirteen before I really came to know that most fascinating of reprobates, Uncle Billy, and the onset of puberty caused me to be more interested in his sexual athletics than his outlandish hobbies. He must have been nearly eighty at the time, and most of his dog-fighting, cock-fighting, whippet-racing cronies had either been hanged or had died of a peculiar brand of defiant senility. Billy still kept game birds, fiery dark cocks and neat, tight-sitting hens, who were the bane of cats and small children foolish enough to venture near a hedgerow where they sat and guarded their clutches of white eggs. I doubt if the old man still fought them, for he, cussed to the end, had out-lived all his cocking friends.

The dictum that the good die young is perhaps borne out by the fact that Billy expired aged ninety-three after a drinking bout with an up-and-coming anti-socialite aged forty. Billy quaffed con-siderable quantities of liquor during his long life, though his standing joke was that he only drank to celebrate specific occasions – for instance, the coming of the night. He was not, however, a drunk, but merely a contrary old exhibitionist – the sort of man who, hearing that cannibalism is illegal, goes out and orders a manburger – and in spite of his bloody interests he was not actually cruel. He was, in fact, an extremely compassionate character, who was known as a somewhat crusty philanthropist, though he would have fought any man who said anything good about him.

I can't really remember the reason why my father took me to Uncle Billy's house – normally it was a place that my mother, sensing my wildness, sought to make me avoid, for her list of deadly sins numbered far more than seven, and Billy was inclined to have a complete pack. Perhaps one of our enormous number of

25

relatives – my grandfather was as prolific as a rabbit – had died, and Dad, who was quite articulate and good at tidying up such legal technicalities as who was to have the aspidistras, was sent to sort things out. Billy's place later became very *verboten* ground for me, but this was the first of many visits to the big house in the near-by village.

He was living at that time with an ex-schoolteacher who, alcoholic as she was, had married him and set to teaching the illiterate man to read and write by chalking words on the stone slabs of the kitchen floor. Billy, who was bright but uneducated, and totally illiterate until he was thirty-five, suddenly blossomed out to such an extent that, by the time he was sixty, he was able to discuss such pointless subjects as the philosophies of Descartes, Lenin and Trotsky with my politics-besotted father – though, to be fair to Billy, I feel he would have much preferred to discuss famous fighting dogs and bare-knuckled pugilists. Billy had money, and so in the poverty of a mining village he could command respect and thumb his nose at the chapel-clad convention of the district. It is said that in his youth he had been so wild, reckless and utterly dissolute that an Irish Catholic family used to cross themselves as they passed his house, rather like Transylvanian peasants outside Castle Dracula in vampire movies. Even in his dotage he was a delightful 'law unto himself' person.

We arrived at the big house near dinner-time, called lunch in the more prosperous world outside the valley, and my father set to work with a vengeance, for not only was he a bit unhappy about settling family bereavement problems, but the proximity to opening time may have acted as a bit of a spur. 'Miss Hammond that was', as the village folk referred to Billy's wife, since she had some forty years before lived with Billy for a short period before marrying him and chapel folk always remember such things, set about sorting out papers with my father. Billy, yawning, noticed my interest in the dusty sporting prints, called 'bad taste' by most people, and sensing a developing interest in his hobbies, rather like Mephistopheles discovering an infant Faust, asked me if I would like to see his 'stock'. Stories of his sexual adventures whispered in school lavatories flashed through my mind and I wondered what he meant by 'stock'. It was chickens that he was discussing, however. Under a dark-green laurel bush sat a dark or Aseel game-hen.

'What do you call these, Uncle Billy?' I stuttered, as the hen shuffled her eggs under her, rather as a fat old woman shifts her midriff before sitting down on a bus.

Billy explained that they were a strain of Aseel game-fowl called Gan, which in some Indian tongue meant 'sledge-hammer'.

'Why sledge-hammer, Uncle Billy?' I went on, like the youth in Lewis Carroll's 'Father William' (and like the youth I was due for my just deserts).

'Fetch an egg out from under her,' said Billy, 'and I'll show you.'

I reached down to the sitting hen and received a stabbing blow from her beak – a blow that numbed my hand and raised a nasty weal across my knuckles. I yelled and looked up.

'See why now?' he said, pragmatically.

Julius Caesar, on making an inventory of things worth stealing from Celtic Britain, writes that the natives regarded the flesh of chickens and also eggs as forbidden food, but in an aside mentions that the Celts kept hordes of chickens just for cock-fighting. We have, as a nation, been regarded as 'bats' by every foreigner from Hanno to Brigadier Gerard. Cock-fighting was little short of a craze in the Middle Ages, and such a respectable pursuit that public schools declared cocking holidays, which must have been a damned sight more interesting than sports day in a modern comprehensive school! It was truly the sport of kings and also, what is little known, very big business. To keep the real McCoy stock and to maintain the blind courage of the cocks – a courage which would allow them to continue to fight long after they had received wounds that should have killed them – rich sportsmen would distribute or walk several hundred or even a thousand cocks to farms around the country. In fact, the walking of cocks was often a condition of tenure of many farmers. Game-cocks need absolute liberty to develop properly, and even young birds will prefer to roost in trees rather than enjoy the claustrophobic safety of being penned up for the night. Of course, the mortality rate is high – foxes pick up the unwary hen or so during the day, and stoats and weasels can play havoc with young chicks, but by the time the game-chick is six months old, woe betide any rat or stoat foolish enough to fancy a chicken dinner.

I had some indication of this fighting ability and do-or-die attitude only a few months after getting to know Billy. Just after the war, when meat rationing was at its worst, the valley dwellers in South Wales took to keeping pigs along the steep sides of the hills. The sties were drystone walls, built for free from the quarries along the mountainside and frankly pretty nasty. Yet public health inspectors were still rare in those days, so the fact that these walls with their myriad long passages crawled with rats often went unnoticed. Farms can, in fact, still be fairly nasty places to this day, for whereas kennels are now subject to public health inspection, battery-hen houses and piggeries in such a state that they would revolt any sane person are not. These stone walls were a haven for rats, and I spent many happy hours ferreting them out and killing them with sticks and dogs.

Near Uncle Billy's place was a fairly large, particularly ill-made piggery where I had permission to ferret and work my dog. Its owner was called Will Northman by the South Welsh natives, who would never let him forget his North Welsh ancestry. Antipathy between North and South Welshmen used to be fairly great, to such an extent that there was a saying in my village that the only difference between a North Welshman and a pig was that you could use a pig when it was dead, a North Welshman being no use alive or dead. Anyway, I liked Will Northman, though I admit his wife frightened me. She had a lard-like pallor and a double row of malformed teeth like a great white shark. Northman had a litter of pigs and I decided to rid his sty of rats, but not before he had moved his large white sow. Sows with piglets are very protective and dangerous. Will (his real name was Bevan, I think) drove her outside, and I set to work ferreting the wall.

It was great sport, spoilt only by the rumbling and crashing of the sow as she sought to get back to her litter. I tried to ignore it at first, and then to my horror the rushes made by this juggernaut of pork began to dislodge the iron hinges loosely cemented into the drystone wall. I was never a brave lad, so I rapidly thrust my ferret into the carrying bag and prepared to vault out of the sty. Too late! She smashed down the doors and, rushing across the sty like an aerodynamic blob, savaged my backside as I leaped out. Laugh not, reader – the bite from a pig is tremendous. My father's cousin, who lived ten miles away had only one hand – the other having been bitten off by a sow who snatched a sandwich out of the boy's hands (he was three at the time). I bled like a pig (no joke intended) and decided to get to my nearest relative, who just happened to be Uncle Billy – then top of my mother's forbidden relatives list.

The moment I arrived I flung down the ferret bag in his garden, locked my dog in his outside loo (his Staffords would have ripped it in two otherwise) and, nearly fainting through loss of blood, staggered into his house. Within minutes a doctor was treating my mangled backside, and pronounced that though it was badly lacerated I would be none the worse for the experience. I tottered out to fetch my mongrel and ferret bag so that Uncle Billy could drive me home. Horror of horrors, my sack was empty, for my white jill had crept out of a tear at the bottom. I had visions of her hacking to pieces Billy's ornamental fowl and went nearly frantic. Heedless of my wounds, I raced up the steep garden. The familiar stench of a frightened ferret assailed my nostrils. There, like two boxers waiting for each other to drop their guards, was my jill and Billy's Aseel cock. My jill was already badly damaged, and in spite of her threats and hissing, the cock dropped his wings to cover his vital leg muscles and struck at her time and time again. I tried to drive him off, but he relaxed his attack only long enough to attack and spur me before resuming his onslaught on the ferret. When at last I managed to get him off he had reduced my jill to a very dead mess of raw flesh. This is all the more amazing when one considers that a ferret is simply a tame polecat and the word 'polecat' means 'fowl cat' or 'poultry killer'.

Early cock-fighters guarded their strains carefully and were reluctant to introduce new blood, even blood that had been tried in the fire of the cockpit. To preserve the courage and purity of the stock, half-brother, half-sister matings were very common. Feather-to-feather matings were always adopted, black-red cocks to their partridge-coloured female counterparts, greys to greys. Piles (a pied colouring, nothing to do with any unpleasant complaint) to piles, duck wings to duck wings, and rigorous selection for both type and fighting ability was adopted to ensure that the bloodlines were kept pure. The Anglo-Saxon at home and abroad adored his feathered furies, and America nearly adopted the game-cock as its national emblem – the bald eagle only winning by two votes.

British farmers, hell-bent for the tropics and similar white men's graves, took their game-cocks with them, as the cocks were bold enough to go for hawks and even eagles that attacked the flocks.

Accounts of game-cocks killing snakes abound, the feathers probably buffering the poisonous bites. Stories of cocks attacking servals and caracals (though doubtless not surviving the folly of attempting such an onslaught) are so common that they have to be believed. English game-birds were the best in the world – or so we thought. We were to be proved wrong, however. Wellington, bent on driving Napoleon from Spain, allowed his troops to take fighting birds with them. What the heck! War was a colourful, macabre joke in those days – didn't a button salesman from Yorkshire find himself smack-bang in the middle of the battle of Waterloo and oblige by carrying messages? But to return to the cocks: our birds were annihilated by the Spanish game bred by peóns for generations and rarely conditioned, as were the English birds, on spices and sherry a day or so before a contest. We returned victorious against the French but losers against Spanish game-birds.

By the time the din of the Napoleonic Wars settled, Britain had conquered more than half the world and the East had all manner of exotic fighting game to offer. Military gentlemen, a-soldiering in India, brought back the hot-blooded and splendid Aseel. (There is a mystery as to how Billy obtained his Aseel birds as our only connection with the army was that we had a relative shot for desertion at the Somme or Passchendaele.) The Aseel (the name means 'noble' in Punjabi), which were powerful and could deliver stinging wing-thrusts and sledge-hammer beak blows, were spirited but not particularly exciting to watch. Many Indian cockers fought their birds unheeled (not wearing spurs), and the battles went on for hours, but these contests lacked the curious ballet-dancer elegance of the English game fowl.

Malay game, fast and furious though greatly outweighing the native British game, also became available, though they were rarely fought in England. The Malay may have looked every inch the grappler (many were over ten pounds in weight), but as often as not, during a 'rest', where the furiously working cocker sought to massage and staunch the bleeding of his ward, the Malay became aware of his stinging wounds and was reluctant to resume battle after the breather. The Malays (people, not birds) were great cock-fighters, winning and losing fortunes on the outcome of the contests. The term 'running amuck' comes from the Malay expression *meng amoq*, a state of mind when the Malay who had lost all his money at a cocking match took a sword or other piece of equipment and set about everyone and everything.

Perhaps the dirtiest trick ever played in cocking was when fighters brought in henny game. The henny cocks, quite distinct from the gaudy cocks of other strains, were drab and colourless, displaying none of the brilliant feathering one associates with cocks (hence *henny* cocks) and were coloured exactly like hens. Story has it that when the henny cocks were first pitted against the normally coloured gaudy cock-birds, the normal-coloured birds fluffed up their feathers to court the strange-looking 'hens' who, far from accepting their amorous advances, delivered a killing blow with their heels. Whether there is any truth in this is questionable, though most books repeat the tale. Normal cocks, stripped out ready for battle, usually have much of their gaudy plumage removed and would themselves resemble a hen cock in this condition. Certainly records do not attest that the hen cock was entirely victorious against other cocks. In fact, very few hen cocks seemed to make the big-time tournaments and now are rarely seen. Few shows, if any, stage classes for these strange-coloured fowl.

Early game-cocks were fought with natural spurs, and the contests, though long and grisly, were seldom spectacular, though they must have offered ample scope for the most ardent sadist. In lengthy contests there is also a tendency for birds to develop what is known as an 'order of peck' and for the weaker to give way to the stronger and 'run', for few contests of strength in nature will continue to the death. No animal living wild without restriction will attempt a battle to the death, for either sexual or territorial reasons. Most give ground as soon as the smallest hint of supremacy is hinted at, let alone established. Even when man interferes with nature by breeding from the most vicious and psychopathic birds, few will fight to the death in an unspurred battle. My own stag game-fowl (young cocks not fully matured) indulge in nasty skirmishes, but none has ever been slain as a result of them. I suppose this is why the metal spur came into use, for the amount of damage done by needle-sharp spurs would surely produce at least a death or two to satiate the savagery of their owners.

Different countries used different types of spur. The Malays fight with a double spur, a naturally positioned needle-sharp steel spur and a spur beneath the feet – a razor-sharp piece of savagery called a *golok*. Both resemble tiny sword blades sharpened to great keenness and held in position by yards of silk thread. A man who can affix these spurs properly can command a high price at an Asiatic cock-fight. Malayan contests are usually over well within a minute, sometimes after the first clash of spurs, for the cocks, weighing over ten pounds, strike at each other with great fury. The rapidity of the contests is possibly why English cockers believe the Malay game to be a cowardly and skulking one. The bird just isn't bred for the long contests beloved by Anglo-Saxons. Malays are deadly in the lightning-quick *golok* contests, however.

The English spur is another matter, and even if one is decidedly anti-cock-fighting one must still admire the artistry and craftsmanship that goes into these exquisite instruments of death. Unlike the Malay spur, which is simply a miniature sword blade, the English spur is a curved piece of steel tapering to a needle-sharp point. The beauty of the construction lies in the nature of the alloy, which does not break or bend even in the stress incurred during a really savage cock-fight. Spur making was once a great art, and the composition of the alloys reputed to be carefully guarded secrets, such secrets that when a maker died he frequently took his formula with him to the grave. Vast sums of money were offered for the formulas of different spurs, particularly the alloys that constituted silver spurs, which were far more highly prized than ordinary steel spurs. Frankly, I am convinced that so much dross and waste must have gone into the metal during smelting and moulding that it would have been impossible for even the maker to reproduce the exact composition of successful and deadly spurs every time.

The noted Clay family, father and son, were perhaps best known for their unique silver spurs, one pair of which was actually purchased by Nell Gwynn as a present for Charles II. Steel spurs, when properly made, also fetched a good price (£3 a dozen pairs when money was really money). Kendrick of Redditch made some excellent spurs, exquisite in the horror of their construction, for they were curved so that not only did they penetrate well but cut on the way out. Ross of Bloxwich had quite a reputation for making really good-quality steels of medium length, so strongly built that they rarely snapped, even after the most exacting contests. Some ten years ago I picked up a pair of Ross spurs in a junk-shop in Tewkesbury, and one could not but admire the artistry in the construction. I kept the pair about two years, and lost it only in a stupid endeavour to find work for it, the story of which I will relate later.

Chicks were taken up for training and 'processing' when they were known to be obviously cock-birds. The combs and wattles were clipped off with a pair of curved scissors, the whole operation being known as 'dubbing'. This seemingly pointless mutilation was not as pointless as appears. First, a cock fought with comb and wattles found itself at a serious disadvantage, for these appendages bled badly when cut, and in the case of comb wounds, the blood poured into the eyes, thereby blinding the cock at the time when he needed all his faculties to ward off the spurs of the attacking dubbed cock-bird.

At between eight and ten weeks old, most game-cocks with the real-McCoy blood start shaping up to each other and fighting. To pen these young warriors or even to restrict them would often result in savage fights. Aseel game, though they mature slowly, are particularly bad when confined. Even Aseel hen chicks fight in deadly earnest and sometimes kill each other when penned in small runs. These young stags were normally put out to walk with a local farmer with maybe half a dozen hens – enough to ensure that he was keen and masculine, but not enough to exhaust him, for a cock's virility is proverbial and a young stag will quickly wear himself out mating a multitude of hens: young and excited, he will tread his hens every few minutes through the day. Most native domestic poultry have game-cock blood as a result of infusion of the blood of cocks at walk.

At two years of age the cocks were taken up for a brief conditioning period. Cocks at walk were fed little, for it is bad to overfeed game fowl, and they had to forage for a good seventy per cent of their food. During walk they had also fought half-hearted battles with other cocks and learned a certain technique to go with the instinctive desire to fight. Then their natural spurs were bound up with cloth and the cocks allowed to spar with retired battle-cocks, cocks that knew the game backwards, in the hope that the youngsters would pick up a few pointers. Few, if any, cocks were fought spurred more than five times in their lives, for apart from the dreadful crippling lacerations inflicted by the spurs, battle-cocks learned to allow another bird to come to them and then to finish him off with a quick display of steel heels. Some cocks learned to kill in the 'shuffle', as the Americans call it, that usually preceded the strike. The wounds inflicted by spurs have to be seen to be believed, but what is more remarkable is that cocks will fight on long after their vital organs have been severely punctured and lacerated. Cocks of the daffodil strain were reputed to fight better after they were blinded – and one shudders to think what horrors this legend must have triggered off among the cocking fraternity.

Old-time cockers fed their birds a special diet just prior to battle. Cock bread, made to a weird and often secret formula consisting of sherry, spices and flour, was reputed to provide that extra 'something' that might make a losing bird a winner as stamina started to give out. American cockers – the sport is still legal in many states of the U.S.A. – use very strange compounds during the last days before a battle, and some companies even manufacture chemicals to induce clotting of severe wounds, thus allowing a cock to finish a battle – before expiring from thrombosis or such like, no doubt! American cockers have explored the art or science of cock-fighting thoroughly, and cocking courses, apparently very scientific courses at that, are run in many states. Science has shown that far from assisting a cock to do battle, cock bread, strangely rich after the cock's scant rations at walk, causes severe digestive problems and actually weakens the bird, putting him at a severe disadvantage during a fight. (Having once boxed three rounds while suffering from dysentery, I know just what they mean!) Many noted American cockers advertise the secret of their 'last days' training and diet, called 'keep' in America, but frankly these strange chemicals and elaborate feed are totally unnecessary. A cock allowed total liberty at walk and given a reasonable amount of food will fight as well as a cock fed on esoteric mixes. The secret is in breeding not feeding, and the most scientific diet will not make a loser a winner.

Blood – or good breeding – is vital, and it is this which makes a real fighting bird: stock bred from battle-torn warriors mated to their half-sisters or mothers, ruthlessly culling 'runners' and stuff of poor type. One often hears uninitiated pseudo-countrymen boast that they have a Leghorn or Rhode Island red which would whip any game-cock. Skirmishes around a farm may look spectacular, but they are no indication of a cock's true courage.

When a cock has to face the frightful lacerations put in by spurs and has the spunk to battle on, that alone is the true test of pure guts. Stories of badly wounded cocks spurred through lungs, guts and aorta, battling on though choking on their own blood and finally dying on their opponent's corpse, are legion. In 1874, a cock of the noted Coathes strain – famous fighters and deadly with their heels – weighing in at 4½ pounds, flew half a mile to kill the master cock at a neighbouring farm and then flew home, and all done with natural spurs. This alone is proof of the saying that it is not the size of the cock in the fight but the size of the fight in the cock. Only a fool will sell short the real old fighting blood, or even underestimate its courage.

In the mid nineteenth century, the noble or ignoble (depends on the way one looks at it) sport of cock-fighting became illegal, and to all intents and purposes the reader may reasonably assume that it is no longer practised in England. A visit to a tinker site, however, will quickly convince anyone that it is anything but dead – better still, if any reader cares to visit Barnaby Fair, they will find the sport practised quite openly. Travellers usually make no bones about what the birds which wander beneath the wheels of their caravans are used for. At the time of writing I breed game-cocks and am continually pestered by tinkers and gipsies alike for birds. Travellers, who to any countryman who has travelled much beyond Bermondsey are a scourge on the country-side, still have the ability to spot a likely game-cock. These people are rarely troubled by the R.S.P.C.A. or police, and they fight their birds with impunity. Time now to correct another romantic theory. Many people believe that the tinker is a source of trouble in the country and the true gipsy is not. This is absolute rubbish. In 1974, a band of Romany-speaking gipsies settled near my village and caused more havoc than any band of tinkers that has ever passed through. We still talk of those frightful ten weeks to this day   end of sermon.

Why, therefore, is your author, a man who professes to be a hunter and to abhor pit sports, eulogizing on the game-cock – or more precisely, why has a chapter on cock-fighting been included in a book of this ilk? Well, thereby hangs a tale – albeit a lengthy one. At the time when I developed an interest in cock-fighting I was teaching in a small, snooty, secondary-modern school in the north. It was the sort of place where elderly drop-out teachers went to die – a kind of academic elephants' graveyard. My bizarre interests and wild enthusiasm for everything met with much disapproval, and I was regarded by the head as a sort of flat-chested Jean Brodie. He was a very weak man and overawed by any woman member of the staff who was in any way worldly or far-travelled. Such a person was Jenny Southgate. She was about twenty-four at the time, and had been there nearly a year when I lied myself silly at the interview and got the job, but she had become a firm favourite with the head simply because she was worldly – and boy, was she worldly! She was viewed with silent suspicion by the elderly members of the staff, who were so xenophobic that they regarded anyone from south of Sheffield as a dago. Frankly, when you really got to know her, Jenny was a bit of a bore, always going on about her adventures with Portuguese fishermen she had met on her latest 'sunshine holiday' (I hate that expression). If you had accused her of hanging around Grimsby docks trying to pick up trawlermen, she would have slapped your face, but she was a real pain in the neck about her adventures in Portugal. If she told the truth, the sardine fleet must have waited off-shore until her holiday was over, fearing to come into port while she, like a Moorish corsair in knickers, ravaged the mainland for any man smelling vaguely of fish.

I had slunk into obscurity beside this woman, and was generally minding my own business and doing a bit of poaching on the side to supplement my salary. I had hunted some fields about ten miles from home and was ferreting rabbits, taking the ones that slipped my carelessly laid nets with a lurcher bitch. I became only aware of the landowner's presence when my bitch was suddenly bowled over following a deafening explosion near by. The swine had peppered her. I was about to shout something offensive when I received a burst myself. My anorak was full of holes and a few pellets had drawn blood on my back. I began to erupt into fury until I saw to my horror that he was reloading his gun. Could he be maniac enough to want to put me out of my misery? Discretion is ever the better part of valour, and I raced off with my bitch limping after me. I turned round, watched him rip up my nets, and for no reason whatsoever shoot my gentle hob ferret at point-blank range. He was a powerful local councillor, so I avoided going to the police – anyway, I was poaching the land. But smarting with defeat I vowed revenge. I cleaned up my lurcher bitch, who was not as badly hurt as I feared, and began plotting.

To wipe out his stock of rabbits would have been easy. All I had to do was to 'lamp' the place fairly regularly with torch and lurcher after dark and he'd have no rabbits to shoot by the time of the next full moon, but I knew his interests were not in rabbits. My enemy had put down a stock of pheasants, and these would make my prime target. They would be easy enough to kill, but to take them with panache to heal my wounded pride –well, that was another matter. I remembered reading somewhere that a game-cock, heeled and trimmed, if thrown among feeding cock pheasants would wreak havoc, for the cock pheasants, angered by the presence of a rival, would attack him; totally unaware of his deadly cutlery.

Well, I had the pair of Ross No. 3 spurs purchased cheaply from the Tewkesbury junk-shop, and now only needed to get myself a game-cock – which was ridiculously easy. At that time I knocked around with a renegade who kept and fought black/red game-fowl. Hardy was a real dyed-in-the-wool Yorkshireman; but he had been born out of place in time. He haunted tinker sites looking for opponents for his fowl, and only the most unwary, or maybe a newcomer, would take him on. I approached Hardy with my new poaching theory. He was not impressed.

'You silly bugger – they're a different species. A cock pheasant will know soon enough that a battle-cock is no threat to his hens. Forget it. Anyway, do you think any pheasant is daft enough to face steels?' he sneered, spitting in disgust.

I persisted, and he eventually agreed to lend me a bird. Alfred, his ancient game-cock, was sire of most of the scrapping blood in the north. He had fought six contests, and the proof of his fighting ability was that he was still alive. I was very hopeful about using Alfred, for his multicoloured plumage was closely similar to the feathering on a cock pheasant, so he must inevitably be seen as a rival, I thought. As a veteran fighter, seven years old to be exact, he knew how to use 'steels' as well as any cock alive. I felt quite jubilant about using him, but to get the pheasants to feed was my next job. I began to spread wheat near a scrub-oak grove, and after four days the pheasants were feeding there regularly.

The day came when I steeled up Alfred, put him in a basket and set out to inflict red ruin on the feeding pheasants. 'Different species, you silly sod,' was Hardy's fond farewell. As I arrived at the grove light was breaking and I watched the pheasants flying in to feed. I reached into the basket to fetch out Alfred and received a stinging peck for my troubles, but the thought of taking two or three pheasants made me ignore minor aches and pains. I took him out, his steels glittering evilly in the morning light, cried havoc, and flung him off. He landed among them, and they flew up a few feet in the air before resettling.

'Sic 'em, Alfred,' I hissed.

Alfred shook his feathers and began to feed. So did the pheasants – totally ignoring Alfred. He was also totally oblivious to them, though he did manage to crow once in boredom rather than challenge. 'Different species,' Hardy had said. 'Ah well, can't win them all,' I thought, and emerged, scattering the startled pheasants, who flew off. So, alas, did Alfred, and settled in a high oak tree. I climbed to recover him, feeling very naked chasing a spurred cock on a game estate. As I reached him, he casually flew off to another tree. I spent the whole day chasing him, but to no avail, and night-time found me bereft of my charge. I limped home, terrified to face Hardy, but he was not particularly upset. 'Different species, you silly sod,' was all he said. I never saw Alfred again. Some fox probably took him, for, in spite of his spurs made by Ross of Bloxwich, he would have proved no match for Reynard.

Yet interest had been kindled in me now, and I began to take the horrific American magazine called *Grit and Steel* – a 'no bones' magazine about 'to-the-death' cock-fighting. This all-consuming interest was to be my undoing. I began taking the magazine to school, and this tended to needle Jenny quite a lot. I mentioned that cock-fighting was still practised in Portugal, but it did no good. She was not only a passionate xenophile (lover of foreigners), but an ardent anti-bloodsport fanatic. Enmity was building up rapidly. It had started when she had joined the local dramatic society who were playing *Macbeth*, but the society's funds had been low, so Jenny asked me to make the swords, at a cut price, of course. I bought strips of mild steel and worked them in the school metalwork shop after the kids had gone home. When I finished, she took them and brazenly told me that the dramatic society had to make 'cuts' and I would not be paid. To add insult to injury, she brought them to school for me to burnish the blades free of rust-spots the night before the production. I became very malicious if hurt, and very childish as well – a fearful combination! I took the swords and edged them to razor keenness before returning them. That night the last scene had an unheard-of authenticity. Jenny was furious and promptly reported the fact that I had made the blades in school to the headmaster! It was the beginning of a permanent rift. *Grit and Steel* probably opened old wounds (ouch!).

One dinner-time she could stand it no more. 'You bloody sadist,' she screamed, threw my beloved *Grit and Steel* on the staffroom fire and flounced off to teach good old 5b all about Bismarck, who, if I remember rightly, once said that political issues were not settled by treaties but by blood and iron. There's a paradox there somewhere, I believe.

3 The Bird-catchers

The peculiar thing about stutterers is that, while they are conversationally incoherent, they are often able to sing with great clarity. Such was my case. My stammering was fairly drastic by the time I was twelve, so much so that it must have been quite a job for any child or stranger not to burst out laughing in my face at the sight of my twitching and the sound of my impediment. I really must have appeared the village idiot to most people. I was, however, able to sing, and like all Welsh schools ours plugged Welsh culture and eisteddfods to such an extent that most of the children would have willingly widened Offa's Dyke, leaped across – and taken out English citizenship!

They were fearful affairs, these school eisteddfods, always opening with an address by one of the governors, a woman with a ridiculous feathered hat that made her look as if a mallard had crash-dived into her hair, and culminating in a particularly nasty Shirley Temple type of girl reciting 'Yr Bugan Brin' ('Scarecrow') by I. D. Houston – probably my cue line, for I was the most shabbily dressed child in the school. The staff, probably equally bored, stood like sentinels by the doors to prevent habitual truants and music lovers from escaping. I would do literally anything to avoid these culture-slaying sessions, but was bullied into singing in one in 1949. I remember it well, for one reason only – the song was the Bird-catcher's aria from Mozart's *Magic Flute*, and it began:

> Now tell me, did you ever see
> A stranger kind of man than me?

Mozart, dying as he did at the age of thirty-five, probably never had time to leave the keyboard, let alone dip his fingers in a jar of birdlime, but he surely knew at least a little about that most strange of men – the bird-catcher.

I suppose the golden age of bird-catching must have been early Victorian times, when thoroughfares like St Andrews Street, London, sold rats nervously cleaning themselves, unaware of the horrendous fate that awaited them in the fearsome rat-pits; Macaque monkeys, fresh from the ships at the East India Docks, whose owners had tired of their pets, or more than likely had suffered some harm from the monkey's nasty bite; and hosts of British finches chattering inanely and unhappily accepting their fate, but bitterly regretting their enforced captivity in the grimy metropolis. Blake, wandering through London in the 1820s, had written:

> A robin redbreast in a cage
> Puts all heaven in a rage.

Heaven must surely have been in upheaval, for London teemed with captive song-birds, some thriving, some fretting away, in the restriction of their cages.

The craze for birds in cages died with Victoria, and Edwardian England seemed more interested in visiting France to shoot live pigeons released from traps than watching the bored antics of an imprisoned goldfinch. My father, whose somewhat narrow circle of friends consisted either of half-crazy Marxists back from Spain after a quick tilt at Franco or the decidedly seedy, used to tell of a quaint old man he knew who limed goldfinches in Pencoed, but who was then regarded as an anachronistic eccentric rather than the norm. The revival of bird-catching came during the early 1950s, in spite of the existence of the R.S.P.B., who, though well-versed in the anatomy of birds, are surprisingly ill-informed about the anatomy of villainy. Imported seed once more became available and money came back into the pockets of the working man. Once again the countryside was about to be raped of its seven-coloured linnets and singing birds.

I should make clear that the trapping of song-birds was never really my cup of tea, not for sentimental reasons, but simply because I have never ever kept an animal that was not intensely predatory. Hawks, however, fascinate me, and to catch one, one needs to get to know the birdlimers and mist-netters, for sparrowhawks feed on finches and small passerines, and any

41

birdlimer worth his salt will therefore know the whereabouts of hawks – and if possible destroy them, for they make considerable inroads into the finch population and certainly reduce the trapper's profits. Also, a sparrowhawk will sometimes crash into the sticky birdlime on which finches are trapped like feathery flies in a spider's web, awaiting the return of the bird-catchers, but hawks so trapped are rarely much use to the falconer as they are usually so covered in the glutinous mess that the feathers are invariably harmed and the palaver of cleaning up usually does the hawk considerable mental damage. More often than not the professional bird-trapper – and such people still exist – will have ways of catching predatory birds.

The Dutch were past masters in the art of trapping hawks, for Holland lies on the migration routes of European predators. In fact, there is a village called Valkenswaard, the 'hawk market', where until recently trapped falconry birds could be purchased and were sold to visitors from all over Europe. The village still exists, so I am told, but the traditional trade in captive hawks no longer takes place. Perhaps it is for the best, as it was a particularly nasty business. The would-be hawk trapper would lie out on the plains in his turf-built hut for weeks to secure enough hawks to make a living, and to sit watching the sky from dawn to dusk would addle any man's brain before long. So he enlisted the aid of a useful if most unwilling ally. Among the hedgerows of Europe lives a curious little bird called the shrike – I say curious, not from his appearance, for he is rather dowdy and inconspicuous, but because of his habits, which are, to say the least, decidedly odd. The ancients called the shrike the butcher bird, because of its rather unpleasant ways of impaling small birds, lizards, worms and so forth on thorns in the hedgerows. Lizards and worms form the bulk of this larder, which perhaps serves him well in times of need, but more often than not they are forgotten and rot away impaled on the meathook-like thorns. He is all in all a very inoffensive little bird (unless, of course, one happens to be a lizard), and he has a marked fear of hawks.

The hawk trapper therefore first set about trapping a shrike. He would cage his captive and once or twice a day hurl a goshawk at the cage to terrify the poor captive bird. It was certainly not a very beneficial exercise for the shrike, who could not really be blamed for becoming decidedly paranoid about the whole business and who could now be relied on to scream blue murder whenever a hawk passed overhead. (Nasty? Well, read on, there's nastier to come.) The hawk catcher merely set the shrike outside the turf hut and went to sleep inside. The sight of a hawk passing overhead promptly set the shrike screaming, and the din awakened the hawk trapper, who promptly released a pigeon on a length of line. If the hawk or falcon was hungry, as many are when migrating, he swooped down, grabbed at the tethered pigeon and promptly killed it; but as he was about to dine, the hawk trapper dragged the pigeon towards some nets.

Now hawks are the regular dimwits of the bird kingdom, and instead of releasing what obviously was a tethered pigeon, they merely bound to the carcass more tightly, totally unaware of being pulled towards the nets and captivity. The hawk realized the error of its ways only once it was firmly enmeshed in the nets. If the hawk was not exactly pleased about this, neither was the shrike for that matter, and come to think of it, the pigeon couldn't have been all that happy either. Man is unique among beasts, not because he exploits other creatures – ants milk greenflies, so we are not unique in our exploitation – but because he can devise amazingly dastardly feats of cruelty to capture his prey. But enough of moralizing.

I became interested in bird trapping only after I decided that, where I had failed miserably with baby sparrowhawks stolen from their nests (episodes told at greater length in a later section), I might have more success with an adult hawk or haggard – one caught wild after its wits had been sharpened by the struggle of surviving in a world antipathetic to sparrowhawks. To the uninitiated – and I was among them once – the most likely place to go to get a trapped sparrowhawk would be a gamekeeper since hawks and gamekeepers seem to go together, like chalk and cheese, for while there is enmity between them, both are aware of one another's whereabouts. Certainly, if you required a dead sparrowhawk a gamekeeper would be the man to get you one. In spite of the fact that hawks are protected and seldom adorn a gamekeeper's gibbet, they are still usually shot on sight, and in spite of the evidence (and 'evidence' is a word I use with my tongue in my cheek) to the contrary, most keepers still believe that sparrowhawks, and even the mouse-slaying kestrel, are killers of game chicks. Furthermore, the knack of taking live sparrowhawks is a nearly forgotten art. Pole-traps and padded gin-traps will catch them sure enough, but these traps will almost certainly damage the hawk. I have been offered many pole-trapped hawks (illegally taken) for next to nothing, though not only are they invariably crippled, but the sight of a wild and furious bird with one leg hanging limply induces such a state of melancholy in me that I would avoid having such birds for that reason alone.

So my search for a wild, trapped, haggard hawk led me away from the pseudo respectability of the gamekeepers into the realms of the dissolute and downright seedy and, in fact, into the company of one of the most incredible knaves I have ever encountered – namely, the late Billy Robbins, regarded by many as a dastardly rogue, but accepted by all who knew him as the greatest bird-trapper in the south of England. I had visited his ill-smelling menagerie to request that he would attempt to catch me a sparrowhawk, and was amazed at his aviary. Never have I seen such a collection of British finches. Aggressive bull-finches, aptly named and shaped like fighting dogs, pecked at seeding groundsel heads while nervous seven-coloured goldfinches watched my approach with trepidation. All were singing and all in a remarkable condition; which was even more remarkable when one considered the fact that they fluttered above two feet of compacted bird manure whose bottom layer was so old that it was in a state of near fossilization. In fact Fisons Fertilizer Division would have done well to offer Billy money for his nasty little menagerie enclosures.

It is quite amazing that most bird-catchers keep their birds in appallingly bad conditions, and more amazing still that the birds always look in remarkably good shape – explained, perhaps, by the fact that no professional bird-trapper keeps his captives very long, as he usually has a 'drop' for them before he sets out to take them. A rapid sale is fairly essential for any catcher of wildlife. What was more incredible, however, was the fact that Billy conducted his sales of freshly caught birds quite openly, though he was very reluctant to discuss the trapping of a sparrowhawk, and more than reluctant to take anyone with him on his illegal bird-trapping expeditions. Finches are of little interest to me, however, so leaving my address with Billy, I departed from his 'zoo' and went home. True to his word, Billy caught me my sparrowhawk, feather-perfect, wild-eyed and in a condition that tells the falconer the bird is freshly caught. She was a miracle of paranoid beauty, her legs undamaged by pole-traps, the feathers unsoiled with birdlime and undamaged by nets, How Billy caught her I never did find out, but it was the beginning of a rather fragile friendship with him that lasted the whole of the time I taught in his district. It was also my introduction to the art of birdliming.

Birdliming, or taking birds by using adhesive mixtures is an almost universal practice. New Guinea natives smear the cups of some sort of campanula flower with adhesive to catch the multicoloured humming bird in order to rape him of his exquisite finery that at one time was used to adorn ladies' hats (making them elegant and ridiculous) or to satisfy some pseudo-ornithologist who prefers the artifices of the taxidermist to those of the Almighty. During the Irish potato famine, sparrows, finches, thrushes and blackbirds, together with a variety of other passerines, were limed and eaten by the starving population. Not only is birdliming the most effective and efficient way of catching large numbers of birds, it is also the most easily learned form of trapping. In spite of the spate of stories in 'country' books, usually written by people whose sole contact with the countryside is a walk along Carnaby Street, liming requires but little equipment and an even smaller amount of skill. I must hasten to add that even though the art is today very illegal, it is still widely practised in the midlands and south of England.

Contrary to its name; birdlime is not made from lime or any other chalky material, but is simply a glutinous, sticky substance extracted from twigs of certain trees and plants. Holly, birch and, in America, slippery elm, are the most popular and most commonly used trees, and here I must add that while birdliming is remarkably easy to learn, the preparation of the birdlime requires considerable skill. Most birdlimers keep their recipes secret, and it was only with some difficulty that I managed to extract Billy's witch-brew formula from him. It consisted of:

1 part holly twigs
4 parts linseed
1 part barley – still in its husks

The whole foul mess was boiled together in water for nearly a day, and its volume reduced by evaporation. It was then strained through muslin or gauze and left to cool. It smelled vaguely like the hair oil used by a headmaster for whom I once worked. Not that he was a birdlimer, mind you – one would have needed to take a second opinion as to whether he was alive, let alone engaged in any illegal activity. But to return to Billy's witch brew, the adhesive would last for ages if kept in a cool shed preserved by the oily substances extracted from the linseed. Billy when I knew him was still using tins and jars of the stuff that he had made just prior to the outbreak of the Second World War in 1939.

Fred Jarvis, one of Billy's unwashed and dissolute friends, who in addition to being a bird-trapper was not averse to taking an occasional nip at a live rat in the local pubs to earn himself beer money, used holly bark boiled with duck fat and well-chewed wheat grains to make his birdlime. This was quite effective while fresh, but even after a week or so it smelled decidedly rank – and come to think of it, so did Fred. Both mixtures were usually kept cool, and were warmed up just prior to use. Billy's mix required to be heated, but Fred's mixture, being more liquid, could be warmed by carrying it under the armpits – birds have no sense of smell at all. So much for formula. Now for use.

To get the finches into the area where the birdlime is to be spread, is, again contrary to most 'country'-type stories, ridiculously easy. Ask any breeder of British finches how often they have to drive away wild finches from the aviary enclosures or sheds. Finches are naturally gregarious (except in the breeding season; when they become pugnacious with their own kind), and the sound of a caged finch singing out its little heart through boredom will attract dozens of its own kind. The limer has only to place a trapped call-bird (who must, to the uninitiated, seem a bit of a Judas betraying its own kind for a handful of seed), to attract flocks of finches into the district.

Apart from this technique, all kinds of birds, including finches, sparrows, blackbirds and, above all, hawks, can be lured into a district merely by placing a live owl (or even a stuffed one) under a bush, or simply jessed to a branch. This draws hosts of frenzied birds to the area, all-hell-bent on attacking the owl, or at least threatening to attack by mobbing. Twigs smeared with birdlime will thereupon catch dozens of assorted birds. An owl is, in fact, far more attractive to small birds than a captive finch, and perhaps the only reason why they are not used is that, firstly, they are difficult to obtain, and secondly, that they attract such an immense variety of birds. Bird-trappers rarely have any market for sparrows, thrushes or starlings, and even chaffinches are difficult to sell, so a load of sticky, superfluous birds is not what is required. A call-bird, however, attracts only its own species, or at the most only very closely allied species. (Chaffinch call-birds will sometimes, but only sometimes, attract linnets.)

At first I assumed that the owl attracted hatred because small passerine birds considered the presence of the owl to endanger their species, owls not being impartial to chicks, though continental gamekeepers used owls to attract large hawks such as goshawks simply by placing a huge and ugly eagle owl in an exposed position so that the hawks would come to mob it. Hawks thus attracted were promptly shot or pole-trapped as they alighted on tree-stumps to shout in anger at the owl. Many students of animal behaviour – I am loath to write the word psychologist, a term I usually use in a derogatory sense – believe that the reason for animosity from small birds is that owls are rarely seen in daylight hours, and small birds, having small but orderly minds, will immediately attack the thing 'out of place', so to speak. Again, I am not entirely happy with this explanation. Hawks and cuckoos are often mobbed (though cuckoos could pass for replicas of sparrowhawks as the barring in the chest is very similar). I am inclined to believe, even though there is no scientific evidence, that this mobbing action has something to do with the coloration of an owl or hawk. I have even seen a musket or male sparrowhawk hung up on birdlime trying to mob a stuffed tawny owl – though maybe he was drawn in by the twittering of the small birds as much as by the owl.

A less time-consuming, more haphazard but often fairly effective method of trapping birds is simply to paint the twigs and leaves of a tree with the warmed-up birdlime. Birds then perching on this get the gooey mess on feet and feathers and simply cannot fly because the adhesive prevents the feathers 'floating' the wings. It is a simple but lazy man's method of trapping one or two birds, and it is not very efficient. To make a living trapping small birds – and this is still possible in this country, for many trappers who are brave enough to run the R.S.P.B. gauntlet often do so – one has to be a little more systematic. First, try an experiment – take a band of assorted hunters on a walk and note the things they can tell you. A rabbit trapper will see only rabbit spoor, I will perhaps only note rat signs, while a finch trapper will see finches everywhere. To be an efficient birdlimer one must be constantly watching for signs of finches and finch food: a professional bird-trapper will tell you the number of types of finch to be found within ten miles from his home. The would-be limer therefore finds a field where finches are feeding on, say, thistles, coming in in their multicoloured droves to peck at the seeding heads. Next he will take a scythe and cut down most of the thistles, dragging them away and, if possible, burning them. Next he will lime certain bits of the remaining thistles. The professional will also carry stalks of coarse grass – esparto is undoubtedly the best – and cover these with birdlime before attaching them to the thistles. Thus the adhesive gets on to the wings of the feeding finches, and they are unable to throw off the lime and adhering esparto grass. The bird is now disabled and easily caught. Some limers can pick up eighty or ninety finches at a session using thistles as bait and at a pound a head from no-questions-asked dealers it is good money indeed. Small wonder there are villains eager enough to chance battles with the R.S.P.B. for such gains.

How to remove the adhesive is the next problem to be solved by the trapper. This is usually done by cleaning the wings with paraffin, but in countries where 'liming' is still legal or only slightly frowned on, solvents can be purchased that are far more efficient and do not damage birds with their poisonous fumes. This cleaning of feathers is always done quickly and quietly, for a finch is an excitable little bird and any increase in its already furious heartbeat often leads to death through shock. Also, the professional limer who has no immediate drop for his birds, needs to watch his captives carefully before they are sold. Many finches do not accept captivity at any price and simply pine away and die. Such 'fretters', as they are known in the trade, are immediately released to breed next year's batch of birds. It is useless to treat them – though the Malay trappers give such birds a grain of opium or so and then sell their catches to unsuspecting dealers. Either way, treated or untreated, 'fretters' always die in a matter of a few days after capture. Strangely enough, on release many pick up immediately and return to hang around the captive finches. Other finches simply settle down to a life of captivity and take food on the same day that they are put in an aviary, but any birdlimer worth his salt will always be on the watch for 'fretters'.

Whether or not birdliming or the capture of live birds is raping the countryside of its song-birds is open to question. Nature usually breeds huge reserves of song-birds, many of which do not survive their first winter. The bird-catcher catches up the surplus and thereby probably prevents their destruction by inclement elements. It is not a matter I would like to debate. My National Service, and thirty-two men to a billet, made me feel intensely claustrophobic, so aviaries, with their air of depression, hold no magic for me. Still, I know of two trappers living just north of Cannock who, until two years ago, made a good living trapping and selling finches, and the population of finches in that district is still very numerous.

One Midland 'limer', who I hasten to add is not a professional, once took 104 waxwings when on holiday in Scotland, merely by taking small pieces of esparto grass and strewing them on some ice around a hole from which the birds were drinking. A limer who lives near Pershore often takes huge bags of bullfinches which reguarly make great inroads on the buds of fruit trees. Bullfinches, however, are a bit unsaleable, so few trappers actually go out of their way to look for them. Winter certainly polishes off bullfinches in number, and they, if limed, certainly weather out the winter in the kinder conditions of captivity The morals of this argument are questionable, as is any form of captivity. Imprisonment or marriage would be death to me, I know, and I doubt if the starving wolf envies the collar and chain on the neck of a well-fed dog. Anyway, as I have said, liming is illegal. It is also on the increase. Why?

Quite simply because better adhesives than the old-fashioned birdlime made from holly bark and so on are now easily and freely obtainable. My readers may gasp in astonishment (at least I hope they will), and ask why is it that the law allows companies to sell such adhesives? Quite simply, because they are not sold as birdlime. Rodent lime, the kind that pest-destruction officers smear on sticker boards to take mice and rats, is far more effective than old-fashioned birdlime, and though it is a bit more difficult to remove, it is literally so sticky that few, if any, finches can get away. A substance designed to hold a struggling twelve-ounce rat has little difficulty in 'grounding' a goldfinch. Moves will probably soon be afoot to ban or restrict the sale of this type of substance, but such moves are somewhat pointless. If one sells a man a cooking pot for boiling onions and he boils up his baby, one cannot be responsible for the misuse of a pot or regarded as a party to murder. The lime is made to trap rodents, not birds.

Disposing of quantities of captive birds must always be a bit of a risk. The R.S.P.B. may swoop at any moment, and fines for being caught in possession of wild birds are fairly steep. Again, the law seems something of an ass. An aviary-bred bird should be 'rung' with a tiny ring to show it has been bred in captivity. The law states that birds not having rings cannot be sold, but unrung birds may be shown at cage-bird shows. It would be a very clever R.S.P.B. officer who could say with any certainty that such and such a bird was wild caught and not bred in captivity. Still, the risks are amazingly high, but so are the rewards. Most professionals will be absolutely certain of a drop, however, before they set out to take birds, but one still hears of occasional convictions for birdlimers.

Personally, I never became really engrossed in the art of bird-trapping, though I suppose it could be said that a finch once saved my life, or, to put it another way, saved what little sanity I have. I had met a really attractive young divorcee – a comptometer operator, whatever that may be – and had, despite the warnings of my friends, who were forever lamenting their loss of bachelorhood, decided to get married. Helena was tiny, neat and immaculately dressed, and, on reflection, dangerously orthodox. But I had finally made my choice, and it was home to meet the family, which consisted of a widowed mother and a younger sister. Helena, whom I now laughingly referred to as my future wife, insisted that I should not wear my customary sweater but must put on a jacket before meeting her family; and this, if I could have seen it, was the red light or danger sign. So, feeling very uncomfortable, I drove her to her family's house in Hereford.

I think I behaved reasonably well during the introduction (or preliminary joust), and then sat through the inevitable formal tea and made polite if rather inane conversation with simpering sister and rather hostile mummy, who blamed the collapse of her daughter's first marriage solely on her son-in-law, whom she believed to be an adulterer, wastrel, lout, drunkard, gambler, nutter, and who had so many faults that it seemed surprising Helena could ever have left such an interesting fellow. I felt decidedly uneasy during this tirade, but tried as best I could to be attentive. The meal over, the entire family left the room to do the washing up, a sure sign that I was ready for micro-analysis, not to say dissection.

If I have a bad fault it is that I utilize my very acute hearing and eavesdrop. It is said that eavesdroppers never hear anything good about themselves.

'Don't like 'im', said simpering sister, obviously unimpressed by my eloquence. 'He speaks like something out of 'M.A.S.H.'

'You'll need to tame [I love that word] him, Helena, he's very wild,' said aggressive mummy, who had sent two husbands to their graves, grateful for their release.

'Don't worry, mummy', said Helena, her voice now changing until it was exactly like her bossy mother's. 'I'll soon tame him. I'll soon get rid of those dogs, hawks and ferrets – you'll see."

I suddenly felt the bars closing in and gazed across the room to where a goldfinch (aviary bred, of course) sang madly and aimlessly in its cage. 'Cage-birds,' said Lorenz, 'sing not through joy, but through boredom.' I was all at once reminded of the Bird-catcher in the *Magic Flute*, who, lamenting his loneliness, rather regretted that he could not trap a pretty maid. Walter Mitty suddenly took over and I was granted a quick glimpse into the future. I saw myself caged like my finch, less attractive, of course, but equally bored, spending forty years across the fireside with a woman who would whittle down my interests to nil and make me dress properly; growing old before my time, and, above all, giving up my priceless freedom. I suddenly became aware that I was never going to be ready for marriage, and like the cowardly dog I am, slunk out and drove home.

Stick to catching finches, bird-catcher, I thought, as I headed north to Yorkshire and continuing bachelorhood.

4 *Well, Don't Knock It Till You Try It*

It is said that Henry I died after eating a surfeit of lampreys and that the first example of an industrial dispute was when apprentice boys were forced to eat heron flesh more than twice a week. Truly, we British are the most omnivorous of nations – very much so when we compare ourselves to the Arab or Pakistani. To the general mass of the public, Arabs eat only sheeps'-eyes and the Pakistani opens his tin of Kit-e-Kat and all the world's well. In point of fact all Moslems, be they Arab or Pakistani, have high standards of hygiene and amazingly strict dietary laws. The Jews have a very explicit code of what thou shall and shall not eat. In fact, Leviticus 11 is full of lists of succulent but *verboten* goodies. Thus all orthodox Jews must eschew such delicacies as rock badger (whatever that may be), pelican or owl, no matter how their fancies take them. Paul of Tarsus swept aside Leviticus 11 with the flicker of an eye, declaring all food to be acceptable, provided it is blessed. Thus a good Christian can tuck into a nourishing vulture with perfect peace of mind (so long as it is blessed, of course).

The British are truly gastronomically unique, however, for not only do we gobble down anything British, but tuck with great relish into Chinese and Indian dishes that would revolt any normal Cantonese or Gujurati. We then have the gall to shudder about the fact that the Romans regarded dormice cooked in honey as a delicacy. But not only are we, as a nation, omnivorous *ad nauseam*. We also have several somewhat idiosyncratic views about food. Our pheasants and hares are, before they are eaten, hung until they reach a state of ripeness and putrefaction that would deter a starving alley cat.

53

Sociologists believe that this is a carry-over from the time when man, unable to pull down game, followed on like a bipedal hyaena after the carnivores and obtained often putrid scraps of meat to supplement his meagre seed and berry diet. Could be true, but wait a moment – most poachers and artisan hunters I know gobble down their illicitly taken game immediately it is caught, and it is only the aristocrat, inspired by slightly potty gourmets, who hangs his game till 'moth and dust corrupt'. Might it be that these gourmets are really secret eugenicists trying to thin out the already overcrowded aristocracy by dint of ptomaine?

Ludicrous as the above appears, it pales to insignificance when one examines the next culinary theory. In 1835, the monstrous and bloody sport of bull-baiting was stopped, and stopped suddenly, for the government was not as worried about the opinions of the *hoi polloi* then as it is today (the mob then had no vote anyway). Many apparently educated and sensible men, however, set up a national outcry against the abolition, not because they supported savagery (the Bill was not introduced to stop cruelty), but because many considered that baited meat was far more succulent, and a bull expiring in awful agony amidst a flood of blood and entrails was supposedly more tasty than a beast killed with a pole-axe. Similarly, a hare that has had a long course before its demise is reputedly more tasty than one that has been shot straight off. 'First catch your hare,' says Mrs Beaton – but preferably after it has been galloped to a state of cardiac arrest.

On now to my own omnivorous experiences, and they are many, mainly because I dislike killing for killing's sake and try to find uses for the carcasses of hunted animals, but partly because I am regarded by even my dearest friends as something of a lunatic. My first kicking over of the dietary traces occurred in 1963 when Britain was locked in the grip of one of the most terrifying winters this century. The sixteen acres of rock and scrub that I must refer to jestingly as my smallholding housed a pool of small surface area but enormous depth – it was actually a deep, water-filled limepit. Winter had frozen it so thickly that they could have played a battle scene on it with complete safety. One morning my lurcher bitch and I went out to catch one of the rabbits now starving and running at half weight – fit only for ferret food. It was a hell of a morning, and the snow was frozen so solid that no fresh rabbit tracks could be found. I can remember thinking that it must have been just such a winter which fixed the mammoths under the eternal ice of the Siberia, but my reverie was broken by the sound of fluttering and flapping.

A heron rose weakly from the ice, flew a few feet erratically, and crashed back down on the frozen surface, too emaciated to fly. Claire, my lurcher bitch, ran nervously towards it and stood, nose to beak with the dying bird. The heron gave her a stabbing thrust with its long elegant beak, and then it was all over in a trice, with Claire carrying the dead bird across the ice towards me. An article in the *Shooting Times*, half hating, half praising the wildfowler, stated that nothing looks worse than dead geese in number. To my mind, the pointless death of this elegant bird was equally nauseating, and I started to rate Claire for her disobedience. It was then that I remembered the apprentice strike and resolved to find out why the twelfth-century boys, who must have been well used to kicks and blows, went berserk when fed liberal helpings of heron meat.

In spite of their statuesque grandeur and enormous wing-span, herons are remarkably small birds once plucked out. I put in the abdominal cut to clean out the bird, and the stench that exploded into the room was one of the most revolting I have ever encountered, equalled only by a horrid cess-pit I had in my garden at that time. In a state of malnutrition, it is likely that the entrails of any creature may cause massive metabolical changes to compensate for the lack of food, and the stench was possibly a result of these changes, or maybe herons always smell like this. If so, the apprentice boys had reason to strike. At all events, I was going to test the meat, not discuss it, and now that I had an oven-ready heron I resolved to use it. Oven-ready is not quite the term to use, for herons have a rather nasty reputation for living for maybe sixty years or so, so roasting was a little inadvisable. I therefore decided to boil the bird in a pan of deep water.

I put the heron on to cook and went out into the freezing morning to fetch wood. When I returned the house stank like Grimsby fish market on a hot day. I slunk out, prepared to face the 20° of frost rather than the fishy stench. I returned later to test my meal. It was ghastly. I offered a piece to the cat, who promptly turned away. Well, there were plenty more animals to tempt. Claire sniffed the meat and slunk off as if suddenly aware of the pointlessness of the kill and probably believing that the offering of the foul morsel was something of a punishment. None of the dogs would even look at the mess, so I promptly threw the whole dish into the ferrets. I like ferrets, they are so unselective in their feeding habits. My hob sniffed the vile bird twice and then set to work on the carcass. Next time you are treated so, apprentice boys, I will help on the picket line.

Now on to one of the hoary oldies that sickens any true countryman, and one that I confess I have related in my previous book, *The Working Terrier*. Smart executive townie, out for a lunch-time trip in the country, pulls smart executive Rover into forecourt of country pub where idiot inbred locals sit, supping brain-addling scrumpy and singing madly songs of seventeenth-century vintage. Executive smiles patronizingly and goes into pub. Orders half of bitter and asks the imbecile barman, who looks like something invented by Thomas Hardy on an off-day, if he could supply some sandwiches. Twittering and chattering from the back room, and a tray of sandwiches promptly produced. Executive tastes them and pronounces them delicious. 'What are these sandwiches, landlord?' asks our executive. 'Badger, sir,' answers the landlord, shuffling off to the back room to entertain his customers with a simple earthy song about mallards, which apparently have extraordinary sexual habits (S.A.E. please, reader). Executive goes away and tells his story in his rather snooty local to similar golf-playing executives. Listen not to him, O town dweller, and leave our badgers ungnawed. It is a huge, ugly lie, spread to malign us country dwellers, who anyway fear the food inspectors far more than thunder, lightning and pagan gods. Badgers are large stoats – more docile, perhaps, than their smaller cousins, but totally inedible. One story will suffice.

Ten years ago Gerry Humphries, who now owns a rather posh Midland pub, was hunting a grove with me near my cottage when the dogs began baying in a small shallow earth. We literally scratched away the earth and found a badger locked in conflict with my best rabbiting bitch who had up till now, been rock steady with badger! I killed the boar badger to stop further damage to the dog, who was on the losing side in the battle. Gerry immediately began to skin the carcass for a wall trophy, and after glancing at the dark guinea-fowl coloured meat, I resolved to try to eat my Brock. At that time I worked in a rather pleasant little secondary modern (desperately trying to be a comprehensive), and was on good terms with the domestic-science teacher, who agreed to cook the badger for me. Now I only needed 'victims' to voice an opinion on the quality of the meat, and it ought to be a fairly large test group. I asked a few teachers to try, and three or four, who regarded me as a harmless, premature geriatric, agreed, but I still needed a bigger group to test this *haute cuisine*, so I also asked a group of fifth-form boys. Now this was a very dangerous thing to do, for while a teachers' union will fight like hell to save a staff member who fondles little girls, or even a pederast, any teacher of a child who complains, ''E forced me to eat a badger, mum,' will find himself very much alone. I got away with it, however, tasted the meat myself and silently divided the carcass among the victims. It was disgusting – a cross between oily pork and swan droppings is how I think I described it at the time. I was not alone in my opinion, for most of my test group hurriedly spat their pieces into the waste bin. Only two people pronounced it in any way edible: one of the staff, who is now a local headmaster, and one of the pupils, who finished up in an institution for the maladjusted – an interesting link here perhaps.

We, of the countryside, can therefore solemnly swear that we do not eat badger! However, I did keep the thin slimy oil baked out of that nauscous carcass, for I cherished the dark thought of a possible use for it. At that time I was interested in witchcraft (oh, reader, how truly grateful you must be that I don't teach your child), and many grimoires, or books of spells, state that before witches attended a sabbat or meeting of witches with the devil, they smeared their bodies with bear or badger oil impregnated with such poisonous plant essences as aconite, henbane and atropine (or tincture of deadly night-shade), and were promptly whisked off to the sabbat. Well it was now May Eve, or Walpurgis Night as the European ancients called it, and I had all my goodies well and truly ready to test the qualities of this potent mix. Such plant essences are quite easy to obtain, for in 1953 Parliament, aided and abetted by Gerald Gardner, passed an Act making magic and the practice of magic a legal and recognized religion, and in most big cities 'witch shops' opened where unpleasant things could be purchased. So it was that I resolved to test the process of flying to a sabbat and be the first in modern times to try the powers of these herbs in their oily solvent. Fame at last. I had been waiting years for Shell to stop doing *Guides to Splendid Residences* and start producing *Guides to*

Ghastly Hovels and get myself interviewed, but the chance of testing the witchcraft came first.

I was quite excited, really. Most psychologists/psychiatrists (depending on where you're standing) believe that the whole thing is one big hallucination induced by the plant drugs, and that the witch does not actually leave the house to attend the ritual, but to my knowledge nobody, but nobody, had actually tested the experiment scientifically. At ten o'clock I said good-bye to a woman friend and stripped off in the bathroom. I then began to rub in the nasty, greasy filth, made only slightly less obnoxious by the addition of the slightly pungent herbs. I had just finished greasing myself all over when there was a knock at the door of the cottage. Panic! How does one explain to a late-night caller why one is stark naked and covered in badger grease? I put on an anorak and jeans and slid to the door. My caller was Sally Evans, a former girl friend who had been pushed out of fashion modelling by the Twiggy look which was then in vogue. She stared at my greasy face and feet in amazement. I just had to explain. She nodded sympathetically and uttered her summary of the whole event: 'You're nuts.'

'Come in for coffee,' I said, trying to seem just a little normal. I gave her coffee, and then desperately tried to get rid of her before the witching hour when I hoped to be whisked away, but she had the sad story of her most recent romance to relate and was staying put. Eleven o'clock, eleven-thirty, and I began to feel strange, and experienced a sudden feeling of weightlessness, followed, I'm sad to say, by an awful vomiting and an agonizingly embarrassing bout of diarrhoea. I desperately tried to wash off the mess, which I knew was rapidly poisoning me. Far from being whisked away to a sabbat, I was carried off in an ambulance to the local hospital. Now, if only I could get some bear grease . . .

Let us now return to the culinary uses of the badger. Who was responsible for the perpetuation of the ridiculous story that badger is edible? Personally, I blame Nicholas Cox, who, in 1617, wrote the quaint and curious *Gentleman's Recreation*. Here Cox states that though the badger is not regarded as edible in Britain (how intensely patriotic), it is treated as a delicacy in Germany and Italy, where it is boiled with pears. What a sickening thought, and what prompted poor silly Cox to write such libellous nonsense? Probably the book was intended to be the cause of war with one country or the other or both. A moment though – during the seventeenth century,

Germany was noted for the number of mercenary soldiers it produced, ever ready to fight for any cause in foreign parts. Who could blame them if they were to return home to fat *frauen* happily boiling up poor old Brock with a mess of pears. You lie, Nicholas Cox, you lie.

On now to the fox, which can scarcely be regarded as edible by any sane person. The unspeakable in pursuit of the uneatable, says Oscar Wilde of foxhunters and foxes. Lucas, in his book *Working Terriers*, mentions that a particular race in India eats foxes and their even smellier relative, the jackal. Before I considered eating fox, I decided to test the veracity of Lucas's statement, so I went to a Pakistani restaurant in Birmingham to make my first inquiry. I managed to corner a rather shy Pakistani waiter, who rarely, if ever, smiled, and asked if any of his nation ate foxes. He stared at me a moment, wondering whether to call the police or simply state that fox was 'off' that evening (and then to call the police?) to placate the raving lunatic accosting him. He compromised and said in perfect English, 'I believe you mean the Sikhs, sir,' and left after an almost Prussian bow.

Next week I attended a restaurant owned by Sikhs and put the same question to a smiling Sikh waiter. (It wasn't that he was amused. Sikhs always smile, even when in pain.) 'No, sir,' he chuckled, 'Pakistanis.' Several decades ago, an American senator called Hiram Johnson said, 'The first casualty when war comes is the truth.' Next week the war between India and Pakistan broke out. Clearly both waiters had been preparing for hostilities.

It was midwinter before I decided to sample a piece of Reynard, but it was midsummer before I got round to it. I took quite a lot of foxes that year, but ferret food was short and I needed the fox meat to feed my hobs and jills. So I forwent my taste of fox until late summer, just after the corn was cut. (It is a strange fact that the hunter's year is divided into corn phases rather than months and seasons.) Moses Smith and I were setting snares for rabbits on the railway embankment near my cottage, for the rabbits had created havoc with the summer corn and we were asked to rid the farm of them. Moses, with the eye of the professional, regarded my efforts with disdain.

'Too high,' he uttered cryptically.

I ignored Moses's comment. Perfectionists always irritate me. Moses is so critical and outspoken that he would probably have told

Jesus of Nazareth that he was doing a particular miracle wrongly. One of the reasons why perfectionists irritate me is that they are invariably right. Next morning the dewy dawn revealed five dead rabbits, and in my snare, set obviously too high – a dead fox.

Snaring is quite an efficient and fairly humane method of catching and killing animals, so long as the snare is set properly. I think it was Christina Rossetti who wrote about the agony of a rabbit in a snare. She had probably never seen one, but then a great deal is written by people who don't really understand the subject about which they are writing. I am convinced Keats would never have written 'Season of mists and mellow fruitfulness' if he had seen the mud and dead leaves that autumn means to the countryman. But to return to snaring, when a snare catches a wild animal, the creature reacts by frantically swirling around and quickly garrottes itself. Anti-bloodsport addicts please note: the Spanish government still believes the garrotte to be a humane form of human execution. Foxes become frantic when snared and die quickly – it would be ridiculous to suggest painlessly – whereas dogs who are used to a collar and lead are rarely actually killed when hung up in a snare and accept their situation phlegmatically with the minimum amount of struggle. Cats, alas, do not accept their fate and go berserk, quickly strangling themselves, My snared fox had scuffed the earth around the snare quite a lot, and then expired.

Well, here goes, I thought, as I skinned the fox and viewed the dark-fleshed, sinewy carcass. I cut away the hind legs and washed the meat in salt water, but realizing that the meat still stank, I left it in salt water for a further four hours. It continued to stink, but I had decided to try, so I boiled the legs, throwing in, as a sort of sick afterthought, some onions. A vile stench filled my cottage. Denis Abbott, a close friend, arrived, inhaled, asked the obvious, uttered a terse, 'They'll lock you up, you know,' and left. I fished around in the aromatic broth for a leg – sadly I found one. The taste was very nasty. To be fair, the anal glands had probably exploded, thereby tainting the meat, but it was one of those unforgettable tastes never-theless. Eskimo tribes will eat Arctic foxes, but with little gusto. The Arctic fox is very tame, and will approach a man during the summer months when its fur is of questionable value, aware that its flesh is so unpleasant that it is safe from even the hungriest Eskimo. In winter months when its pelt is prime, he becomes decidedly suspicious about Eskimoes and gives them a clear berth. Oscar, you were dead right about the uneatable bit, at least.

Cat meat is another matter, however. During the Franco-Prussian War, when people raided even the zoos during the Siege of Paris and elephant appeared on the menus of fashionable restaurants, cat was regarded as a delicacy – and well it should be. The carcass of a small female cat is very similar to a domesticated rabbit, both in taste and shape, and only if the kidneys are left in can the carcass be distinguished from that of a rabbit's for the kidneys of a cat are level, whereas those of a rabbit are staggered – one higher than the other. I confess I like cats (not in a macabre sense), for I keep a Siamese, but I am also aware that a cat gone wild can be a damned nuisance anywhere. Maurice Burton, a superb naturalist by any standards, believes that something goes anatomically awry when a cat goes wild. An ordinary undoctored tom-cat strays away from home and takes to the woods. Hey presto! Something erupts and his metabolism goes berserk. He begins to gain both weight and size, even though he was an adult when he first strayed from home. Enormous cats are sometimes shot by gamekeepers – and these are not genuine wildcats, but merely domestic moggies that have taken to the wild. Twenty-pound feral cats have been recorded in Suffolk, and I have seen several that would put even a very hard terrier to flight. Such moggies are great pests on any game preserve, for no cat is ever 'rock steady' with small birds of any sort. Thus cats create havoc during pheasant- and partridge-rearing time and are absolutely lethal with small poults. Kipling's cat 'walked by itself', and a damn good job, for a hunting pack of cats would denude the countryside of all wildlife.

Most keepers shoot feral cats on sight, and although I have a great affection for my Siamese neuter, I still have sympathy with any keeper who has to put up with the carnage caused by a hunting feral cat. Ferrets have a 'thing' about cats and enjoy the meat more than they do rabbit flesh. In fact an ailing ferret will often tuck into a road-casualty cat when it has refused all other meat. Feeding cat-meat to ferrets is not without dangers, however, for ferrets can contract deadly feline infectious enteritis from cat carcasses. At one time I fed all cat carcasses to my ferrets, but one day, after a spectacular rat hunt, we had meat aplenty for them. Late that afternoon a gamekeeper friend – I still have friends in that profession – brought a great thirteen-pounder tom-cat that he had been forced to shoot on his estate. Jeff Elwood and I set to skinning the beast with a view to tasting it. Now normally I can skin, clean and gut a rabbit in forty-five seconds, but it took me nearly twenty minutes to skin that old tom-cat. Every inch of his fur was held by manacles of ancient sinew, and we were nearly exhausted by the time the beast was ready for cooking.

When Jeff realized I was serious about eating the cat, he suddenly went a little pale and made a lame excuse about having to be home early. Undeterred by gastronomic cowards, I strove on. The stench of the boiling cat was nasty, and it nearly turned my stomach before I plucked up enough courage to try the first mouthful. Oddly enough, the taste was delicious and nearly indistinguishable from well-grown, commercial, domesticated rabbit. Before the reader scoffs, or is horrified by the fact I have eaten cat, may I remind him that there are nearly a quarter of a million cats in Great Britain, and that many of the strays which sadly must constitute the bulk of the cat population finish up in what is ludicrously known as an 'Animal Shelter' and there are put to death (quickly and painlessly, but nevertheless to death). Is the reader foolish enough to believe that these strays receive a good Christian burial in some feline potter's field? I assure you they do not. They are sold and ground up to make meat-meal fertilizer – ashes to ashes, dust to dust, cats to . . . manure. Let the quaint old ladies who turn loose their beloved pets to a life of feral havoc realize that they stand little chance of being eaten by me, but an exceedingly good chance of finishing up as the rose-bush dressing that they will be buying a few months later.

On now to yet another insane thought. It is commonly believed, and the story is still perpetuated by countrymen who have journeyed into the very heart of wild Surbiton, that gipsies exist only on hedgehog, summer and winter alike, rolling the prickly beasts in clay and baking them in a fire in their resulting jackets. Our Rover-driving badger muncher will no doubt confirm this story at one of his dissertations in his snooty local. One day our executive friend drove his Rover well off the beaten track, and stumbled on to, or rather parked beside, a gipsy site where happy Romany folk, dressed in Romanian finery, were gaily singing songs of Magyar origin, stroking their exquisite lurchers and baking something succulent in a foil of clay. Our traveller was received with cordiality and friendship. He was offered food – again a delicious meat. He asked its origin – yes, you've guessed, it was the inevitable hedgehog, baked according to a traditional earthy recipe (bad pun). Our executive waved good-bye to the horse-drawn caravan dwellers, and was off back to the city to tell his fellow executives, hot from the golf course, just how the other half lives.

So old and hoary is this story that it might as well be an essential part of infant education – cows eat grass, dogs eat meat, and gipsies live on clay-baked hedgehog. Lies! First, the typical Romany (and I live near a site) is suspicious and inhospitable to strangers, referring to them as Gorgios (or outsiders). Furthermore, I have yet to see a hedgehog eaten by gipsies. Moses Smith, an accurate observer of gipsy life, and a settled gipsy himself, says that during his long life he has known few gipsies who were not actually offended by the mention of hedgehogs. In desperate times they were eaten, but never as a staple diet.

I rather like hedgehogs. They are stupid but harmless little beasts, totally unable to adjust to the pace of modern life, so I was just a little reluctant to try one. Not so long ago, however, I was driving back my two part-time kennel lads from an early-morning hunting/coursing expedition when the wheel of the van hit a hapless spiny bundle, killing it instantly. We stopped. My lads were keen to make a gipsy meal, so back we went to the cottage. The fleas deserting the cooling carcass deterred the lads from baking it in the spines, but we set to and skinned the beast, cleaning out its insect-filled, worm-ridden body. We then cooked it. It was revolting, second only to badger.

I will leave this tale of all things edible with one last story. I was in a house in Rotherham some ten years ago when, half-drunk, I mentioned that rodent flesh and rabbit meat were practically in-distinguishable to anyone except a gourmet. When I am drunk I am extremely boring (what the heck, some people are violent), and was coming on with high-faluting quotes from the Pigafetta diary about the fact the Magellan's crew bought and sold rats for a ducat each and ate them to remain scurvy-free during the long voyage around the world. (It should be noted that Magellan did not finish the trip, probably preferring death to diet no doubt.) This was not an uncommon thing. Once the scurvy-ridden crew of a British ship died, leaving only one addled-brained idiot deckhand healthy and scurvy-free. It transpired that he had eaten rats to ward off the scurvy, but nastier still, he claimed to have eaten young ones not only raw, but alive!

I was quoting, or rather pontificating, about my favourite animal, and certainly boring my audience, when someone in the audience asked if I had the courage to consider eating a rat. Of course, I replied, blasé to the last, and felt suddenly trapped as £10 appeared as if by magic in order to call my bluff. I was, in spite of my drunken exhilaration; aware of exactly how Jesus of Nazareth must have felt when asked who the Jews should pay the taxes to, but was unable to come up with a dietary 'render unto Caesar' epigram. Too late! I was called to put my money where my big high-falutin' mouth was, and was forced to take the group on a day's ratting to procure my meal. Oh well, I thought, sometimes a hunter has a dead day and we could, with luck, return 'ratless'.

We arrived at the ratting tip, the dogs jumped out of the van, and to my utter dismay nailed a rat within the first few seconds of the drive. It was a very large and aged buck, very mangy and very, very inedible, bearing all the skin diseases that speak of rodent antiquity. To summarize – a perfectly horrid specimen. I began to pray we'd get another, and that I'd be spoiled for choice, but my luck was out – it was the only rat of the day.

The jubilation of my supposed friends led me to believe that John Donne, writing 'No man is an island', had not been to Rotherham in similar circumstances. I have never seen so many eager and malicious faces, frantic to see me go down with some infection virtually unknown to the bacteriologist, and then dying like Francis Bacon saying something about expiring for science. I searched for an honourable way out, but my pub-mates, knowing my cowardice, had neatly sealed all exits. We returned with our rat, my friends gleefully talking about the awesome bacteria they had heard that rats can carry. As part of the deal I furnished the group with my biological dissection kit, and my friends (and I now wonder why I go on using the term 'friends') set to work to skin the creature. They skinned it in some allotment shed as Henry's wife considered it unfair to clean it in my kitchen, as the occupant immediately after my demise would have a devil of a job disinfecting the house! Friends – I had none. To the last one they all gloated as the rat boiled in an old pan furnished by one of their wives, gleeful that her husband would soon be out of my evil clutches and that her life would return to normality soon after my burial.

I glanced at the pan and its simmering soup, teeming with distinctive dormant microbes, eager to spring to life as soon as ingested by me. I am not ashamed. I faced it like a man. I paid up my £10 without a complaint! Some two weeks after this, a D.Sc. degree was granted to some bright spark who had proposed that the answer to the world's food problem was to feed laboratory rats on compressed sterilized human faeces, and to can the rat meat to sell to starving underdeveloped countries (who would then rise up in indignation, I'm sure). Oh, brave new 'Third World'.

I confess I have also backed down to betting men who have challenged me to shrew/mole/stoat/ferret-eating contests, but before the reader finally slams shut this book in disgust, I mention two facts. In 1754, in Edinburgh, one Nichol Brown went to the gallows after killing, cooking and consuming his wife. Evidence at his trial indicated that he had also roasted the week-old leg of a gibbeted felon over an inn fire before eating it. Jonathan Swift, at his savagely satirical best in his essay 'A Modest Proposal – for preventing the Children of the Poor People from being a Burthen to their Parents, on the Country, and for making them Beneficial to the Publick', suggests ways of serving up cooked infants. Besides such masters, my gastronomic feats fade into insignificance!

5 San

'Christ, you're ugly,' was all I could think as I dug a deep hole and put him in it. It was seemingly a poor epitaph to the best and most loyal dog I have ever owned, but strangely it was as much as I could manage, though I confess tears ran down my face as I shovelled the earth over him. I am forty now, and it is doubtful if any dog will serve me as well or as long as he did. He was, indeed, the most perfect of all my hunting dogs, and though he did have one fault – a strange one at that – he never once let me down or made me look a fool in public. As I write this I look around my tiny bachelor cottage. Most of the house was bought as a result of bets made against me by people who owned 'the best little ratting terriers in Britain' – and all of them were put to shame by the sullen, ugly little dog I buried beneath the apple tree near the spot where I kennelled him when I first came to live in this district. Hunters who are hunters will tell you that one is granted one great dog in one's lifetime. San was mine.

Where should I begin the story of a dog that lived over half my life with me? Well, in true story-book fashion I will begin at the beginning, and the beginning was a long time before I was born. My mining valley was the home of some of the toughest terriers I have ever encountered. Indeed, the Garw was much noted for its working dogs some thirty years ago. Story has it that quite a few years before that several miners went to Somerset. There was a rest home there where tuberculosis victims (my father was one of them) went to recuperate. In due course, these miners returned minus tuberculosis but with two hard-bitten little terriers of the type we refer to as Jack Russells today. These were used as a base for the valley strains.

Tom Evans of Blaengarw says that they were maybe a bit too hard for the 'hunts' of those days, which required a dog to bolt a fox, not damage it or thrash it to death, but the miners were not too worried about the finer points of hunting and didn't consider 'hardness' to be a fault. They were not by any means, of course, the only terriers in the valley. Three streets behind my own terraced house lived a man who had tried to evolve his own strain of working terrier by crossing a small fighting bull terrier with a hard-bitten Bedlington. The offspring, as one would expect, were hideous and resembled blue-black Dandie Dinmont terriers with huge pot bellies and jaws that could bite a hole through a wall. There were possibly tougher dogs than these, but I never knew of any. They were mute, and iron hard, but badger baiting was popular in those days, so dogs that could withstand the fearsome jaw bites inflicted by a cornered boar badger were highly prized, and this strain was used to mate to the Russell-type terriers. The Sealyham – no, not today's show specimens, but the real McCoy bred and beloved by John Tucker Edwardes – was then in the process of creation from an ill-assorted hotch-potch of native terriers, Dandie Dinmonts and a spunky little bull and terrier called the Cheshire terrier. These game little animals also entered into the strains of the valley terriers.

The result of this genetic morass, with a fighting bull terrier or so thrown in for good measure, was formidable in a fight, lethal below ground when worked to fox, and, above all, the finest ratting dogs I have ever met. The lightly built Russell blood gave them timing and agility. The bull-terrier blood, light weight 20 pounds catch weight fighting dogs, gave them guts to tackle and stay with their quarry, and the sundry other breeds gave them something special in the way of nose. They were unstandardized, ugly (though a show-stopper did appear now and again), but as pound-for-pound terriers – well, they didn't have an equal. They were dead mute and many had bad mouths – a legacy of some bull-terrier blood – but they were tough enough to match the devil.

I had owned dogs of this strain before and knew they were utterly fearless, but San came to me with a reputation for being a coward. It seems so strange now that even I find it hard to believe. My valiant-to-the-death terrier arrived at my place with a reputation for being a quitter and yellow; and damned fool that I was, I believed it. I had trained his litter brother, Dusty, whose courage could not be faulted, though he was, to be kind to him, a little short on brains. Or – let's not be kind – he was damned stupid, though on second thoughts it was maybe me, for I just didn't blend with this dog.

Dusty was a good fox killer. Too good, in fact, for I have never seen a dog kill a fox as quickly. He would rush in, impervious to bites, and batter his fox to death. He was, however, like a great number of his family, absolutely mute. Hunting with Dusty was simply a silent subterranean battle which always ended in a very dead fox and a very badly torn dog creeping sheepishly from the earth. The whole strain had this peculiar trait. When they killed a fox, they would creep from an earth as if ashamed of the action.

I never once saw Dusty give ground to anything and never once heard him whimper with pain in spite of the terrific maulings he received. One day, however, he met a boar badger who had a similar disposition, and as the badger weighed 30 pounds and the dog a mere 16 pounds – a sort of irresistible force meeting an immovable object – something 'just had to give'. I dug down to the muffled thumping and rumbling without any great haste, unaware of the tragedy that awaited me. I found Dusty dying, his jaws smashed, his throat laid bare to the windpipe. He died as I vainly tried to get him to a vet. One often hears of men, usually old men, who claim to have owned dogs that would kill a badger. Such dogs are always senile or dead or in some way unable to repeat the performance. Disregard these stories. Dusty was a gallant little brawler, game as a bantam cock, who would put up a hell of a show against anything on four legs. It is sufficient to say the badger slew him in less than half an hour.

So to his litter-mate San, who was a strange dog whichever way you look at it. As a puppy he was fearless, more game, in fact, than his brother Dusty. He was also quick to anger and easy to provoke – all the qualities that usually bespeak a rip-roaring worker. At eight weeks old he had fought a grim, silent battle with his sister – no, not the petty puppy battles fought by babes over trifles, but a jaw-to-jaw combat, the animals locked like two immature pit bull terriers hell-bent on destroying each other. When separated, they screamed with rage to renew the conflict, and the whole litter had to be parted to prevent a death. San was sold to a local hunter and became what is called a 'flyer'.

Now 'flyers' are a lot more of a problem than a dog who is slow to enter, for it is a sore temptation not to push a youthful enthusiast to breaking point. This was how it went with San. At four months old, with his milk teeth still in the process of shaking loose, he had been put in a corn bin with some fox cubs of roughly the same age. This is a brutal, stupid and very wasteful method of entering a terrier to quarry, but it is still practised by many hunters in South Wales. Some of the ideas of my fellow valley dwellers were and are nothing short of ludicrous. It was commonly believed that a terrier who would stand being picked up by the tail without screaming was game, and that certain markings indicated certain qualities in a dog. Such ideas are in fact still widespread. In the Fell districts, a white-footed terrier is frowned on, and many purists put them down, for white feet are supposed to indicate constitutional weakness. There is, sadly, precious little science in terrier work.

To return to San, however, he promptly killed his four tiny adversaries, who had probably cowered in terror on the far side of the bin, hissing and spitting in fear in their alien and hostile surroundings. Yet fear gives just a little edge to a beast's desire to survive, and they must have put up a grim battle against the puppy. Next week San slipped his leash at the end of a badger dig, when the screaming, barking and grunting drove the youngster so mad that he could not resist rushing into the fray. Brock committed mayhem on the adult terriers, and Sam pulled out several of his milk teeth on the hide of a boar badger being worked by his mother and older sister. Such a 'flyer' needs holding back and gently restraining, but it is a wise man who can resist the temptation of pushing such a game puppy to the limit of his courage. The following month his delighted owner put him in a corn bin with an adult vixen, and she thrashed him so badly that he cowered on the far side of the bin, whining and whimpering to get out. It was an obvious 'no contest', and the puppy was ridiculously overmatched. He was thereafter terrified of foxes, and this was why at eighteen months he was passed over to me as a coward and a quitter.

Terrier men are a little like young teachers. Kids straight out of college automatically think that the children they teach are backward, not through any lack of intelligence, but because other people have taught them badly. The first few years of terrier keeping and teaching are therefore a subtle hybrid of disappointment and realization. San took nearly a month to get used to me and to come when called. On the day he arrived he escaped from his crate and I spent several hours chasing the terrified beast through the streets of Shrewsbury. After a month we had become used to each other, however, and a strange bond had already begun to be woven between us, much like a sort of spiritual spider's web. We had so much in common, for I, too, was a failure in the eyes of the world and knew of his problems as he later came to know mine.

Strong as this bond was, it didn't help much in entering. I took him to an uninhabited earth and, sensing an excitement building up within him, let him slip his lead. Instead of crawling into the earth, he raced back to the car in terror and lay cowering under it like a dog that has just received a particularly savage thrashing. Of course I was disappointed – I would be a liar to say otherwise – but it wasn't the end of the world. I returned to the earth, tied him a few yards away and put in a bitch called Puke. In twenty minutes I had my fox, and threw the carcass down in front of San and released him. Again he raced back to the car, fearful lest I should follow him with the hated cadaver.

He was obviously a crass coward, I told myself, now more than a little disappointed at this new introduction to my kennels. I fetched him back and back-filled the shallow earth. We both walked back to the car and I was feeling about as hangdog as he was. We rounded a corner of an old farm building just as a stray tom-cat cut across like a spectre from the farm rubble, gently hissing its warning to the dogs. San hit the cat head-on and a frantic struggle began, ending only when I managed to beat him savagely to allow the cat to escape. I sat down on the pile of rubble exhausted, but above all bewildered. Any dog who will rush a farm cat head-on is no coward, and cat killers are, practically without exception, good fox dogs. This is not surprising, really, for a cat is a tremendous pound-for-pound fighter and instances of a cat killing a man are known. Hence, a dog who will face those needle-sharp teeth and wicked hind claws is either very courageous or a sheer lunatic. What the heck, I suddenly thought, I have other fox dogs. So I decided to 'put him up' for a while, allow him to hunt small quarry, and then, once I'd erased his bitter memories of fox, I'd try him once again. It was to be another two years before I was able to work him to fox, and he was as near as dammit five before I entered him properly.

However, those two intervening years were to be work-filled. I have often thought I'd rather be the world's hopscotch champion than an indifferent middleweight fighter. Well, my dog had refused fox, so I would try him to other quarry – and my first attempt at re-entering him was to be a resounding success. A friend of mine owned a piggery – concrete buildings, apparently rat-proof, but somehow the rats had burrowed beneath the concrete and what proved to be a very large colony was living in the foundations. My jill ferrets were in kindle and I was a little at a loss to devise a method of flushing out the rats. Still, there was a water tap at hand, so I flooded the warrens and the rats floated out on the deluge. San had never seen a rat before, and my team of terriers were all experienced ratters. Yet, as soon as the flood forced out the rats, San was galvanized into action. I have ratted all my life, and have taken over a million rat, but the magic of those few moments will never be forgotten. He killed with surgical precision and with the grace and skill of a ballet dancer.

There is macabre and horrid poetry in watching a skilled dog slay rat. Nasty, but poetry in motion in the same way as the skill of a rapier swordsman, whose pride will allow him to kill only with the point, not the edge. He struck, crunched and chopped with dazzling speed. It was all over so quickly, but then so was a duel involving Cyrano de Bergerac. San worked equally effectively. Thirty rats lay dead, of which he had taken half. I had won 'rat money' with all my five terriers, but even they seemed bewildered by the speed of the newcomer.

Next day, dawn found me putting a friend's barren jill into my ferret bag and heading for the nearest tip. San was stupendous, and though he missed the first two after I rated him for going for the ferret, he soon settled down to the sport and I had to stop him before he wiped out the entire colony, which I had nurtured and fed like some slightly potty gamekeeper carefully encouraging his stock. My next task was to learn his ways, so he moved into the house, and I even let him sleep in my bedroom and eat from household dishes. Not as crazy as it sounds, actually. A hunter really needs to be *simpatico* with his dog to do well. Hence, a man who is forever buying and selling dogs never really gets to know them and never gets the best out of a hunting dog.

As it turned out, San and I really did move on to the same wavelength. We grew very alike – people do get like their dogs – both slightly schizoid, both with moods varying from extreme joy to the deepest gloom; so much alike, in fact, that we began to anticipate each other's actions. He became dangerously possessive towards me, watching anyone who approached and attacking a girl friend to whom I must have shown some affection. He really was the strangest of dogs – rarely showing emotion, even

71

by a wag of the tail, but forever watching with those ever-seeing, 'Laughing Cavalier' eyes. My God, there really was a bond between us, and he became a canine mirror image of me in those months before we were ready to milk the suckers, for it now remained to find a rat-killing terrier's owner foolish enough to bet money on his dog.

We found them aplenty. Nearly every terrier man I know has the best little terrier in Britain, and I was broke enough and unscrupulous enough to take advantage of any owner foolish enough to bet on his dog. Every beam, every tile of my cottage was bought as a result of San's work during these wild days. So fast did he kill that no one, not even the worst loser, contested a decison during those days. I was now travelling twenty miles or more to find clients or victims, but fame of this kind spreads fast and people began to stop being led into boasting that they had the best little ratter in Britain. In one eight-hour shift, when a tip was being bulldozed (and being netted) he killed, in front of fifty-four witnesses, six of them press men, 1,126 rats. I have had no dog who equalled, or come to think of it, came near to this feat. After this achievement his face swelled so badly that it was six days before he could eat or drink, and his weight fell from 16 to 12 pounds, but three weeks later he was back to ratting with his usual enthusiasm.

I began to grow cocky, and started challenging men with two or three terriers, and pride of such a nature and against such odds is bound to come before a fall. However, I was prevented from arriving at financial disaster by the fact that a rather unpleasant situation made me decide it would be expedient to leave the country for a while. So I dumped San with a former girl friend and left Britain. It was two years before I saw him again. He recognized me instantly, which is strange, for dogs forget so easily, and the bond between us, only slightly cracked, became re-cemented, perhaps more strongly than ever. He had seen no work for two years, for while Karen had walked him and allowed him to chase and even catch a few rabbits in the undergrowth around her cottage, her recently acquired husband was a bank clerk and decidedly anti-bloodsport, so the pair were rather glad to say good-bye to both of us. San and I took maybe a week or so to adjust, and we were back in business looking for suckers – truly the spirit of Uncle Billy burned strongly in me, for to this day I cannot resist gambling on any good dog I have trained.

In due course employment took me to Yorkshire, and I won enough money (in a card game) to put a sizeable deposit on a £550 house: the two-up, two-down, variety, shunned by ambitious newly-weds, but more than enough for my humble needs, for I have never really needed a great deal – nor possessed it, for that matter. Anyway, there was still rabbiting to be had on that industrial complex where the towns of Rotherham and Sheffield fuse together to form a huge, sooty metropolis – a grimy, grim, but happy twin town. The wasteland around the works, where the ground was so gritty and poisonous that grass eked out an existence between clumps of fireweed and bramble, held a surprising quantity of game. Originally the game had been trapped by houses as a magician throws a spancel around his victim, but industrial development brought with it a new type of person – a non-hunter, only casually interested in wildlife, so the rabbits, left alone, increased surprisingly, causing interest only when they denuded crops of lettuces in neighbouring gardens.

To the civilized people of Rotherham, I must have seemed the arch-predator, a rather unpleasant, uncivilized sort of relic of a world they would sooner have forgotten. One day I was ferreting on one of the farms that flourish even in the shadows of factory towers, with San marking holes my sloppily placed netting had failed to cover and giving me quizzical 'you damned fool' looks. My farmer friend ambled across with the walk that has been an agricultural compulsory since Tubal Cain. 'Sithee' – most died-in-the-wool Yorkshiremen start a conversation with this word – 'can your terrier shift a fox for me?' Suddenly I remembered San's cowardly reactions in that direction and laughed as I explained to the farmer. He shrugged his shoulders, murmured something about useless dogs (such conversation is usually as compulsory as the walk and 'sithee') and left. I laughed again. I wasn't really worried if he would go to fox or not. He was a superb ratter, a great ferreting dog. To hell with foxes, I thought, and what did it matter if his early traumatic experiences had made him frightened of fox? I had 'earth' dogs aplenty, anyway. I would come back with one tomorrow and deal with the marauder, but today I would rabbit.

The warrens, however, yielded a sparse crop of bunnies, though it was of no great consequence. I worked at a pitifully paid school-teacher's job, but I had enough money to live, so the rabbits were unimportant. I shrugged my shoulders, lifted my nets and moved further down the bank, my terrier sniffing eagerly at the unnetted bolt-holes and nudging my legs if I failed to net them quickly enough. What a priceless ally he was, I thought. Ferret in, solitary rabbit out, and on to the next spot. The next warren, however, stank of fox and the hair on San's spine prickled until he looked like a Rhodesian ridgeback. I watched him, mentally betting myself how long it would be before he ran for home. It was only a matter of time, I was sure. Even after four years he would still remember the awful dusting he received in the corn bin.

San, however, did not run. He stood at the mouth of the earth, sniffing the sides as if to drink in the intoxicating odour of fox and fear, looking for all the world like a ferret who realizes that the rat in a hole has biting powers equal to its own. No, he didn't race for the car, but edged into the earth carefully and pussy-footed. Seconds later, bedlam (funny word that, it was, I am sure you know, a lunatic asylum) broke out as he engaged his fox in combat. At first the baying was a nervous falsetto – a tone created by the memory of the corn bin – but seconds later it became the booming sound of a dog who has decided that the beast within is a worthy opponent and he will engage it. I glanced at the earth. It was a small earth – simply an excavated rabbit warren – but the hawthorn tree on the bank could prove a problem. A fox lodged behind a thick tree-root can create mayhem on a dog, and this would be the last straw if it happened to my newly awoken fox dog.

I took my ferreting spade and dug to him with an unaccustomed frenzy – for I dislike digging – and found him nose to nose with a small vixen whose body was curled up into an amazingly small hole in the tree roots. San stood watching her, giving tongue venomously if still a little apprehensively. I dislike any form of baiting. It is brutalizing to the man, dangerous to the dog, and the quarry usually doesn't care much for it either, so I tied San up and drew the fox. Foxes are easily killed with a sharp blow, and killed painlessly at that. A noise startled me, and I turned. The dog was going into paroxysms of rage – pulling at the lead to worry the dead fox. He attacked the body madly, well and truly wed to the quarry – or apparently so, but I am a little suspicious of one-swallow summers, for he had much to forget and even more to learn. Seemingly so did I, for I took the greatest risk any terrier man can take. I tried him at a 'hunt' meet.

Next day I went to the neighbouring fox-hunt pack, the terrier

75

man for which was a close friend of mine. It was the day of the meet, but then nearly every day was, for they hunted five days a week. Hounds and horses were milling about like a Christmas-card scene. The overheard conversations of the riding-to-fox fraternity are usually extraordinary.

'Well, I tell you, he's at that difficult age.' Question – puberty or male menopause. I've always been at that difficult age.

'I hear Godfrey is home from Eton,' says a portly lady, whose enormous backside is weighing down a lightly hunted 16′ 3 hunter groaning under her avoirdupois. Godfrey is evidently home having learnt to say, 'Pass the marmalade,' succinctly, and, after a spell in the Guards, to have his picture in the fashionable country paper – front page, next to the stud advertisements for stallions.

A young, eligible lady yawns – I lose interest in her, for just as people get to look like their dogs, so do equestrians get to resemble their mounts. But we are ready for the off. The Master goes past, lightly touching me with his riding crop. I do so like that, it makes me feel wanted! The hounds draw cover and away goes the fox into a field of kale. I am suddenly struck by the awful damage a pack of hounds can do to arable land. The whole area soon looks like a dance hall after a party of Welsh miners has left. Could the death of one solitary fox, I wonder, atone for damage of this scale?

I was snapped out of my reverie by the huntsman blowing 'to ground'. Philip, the terrier man, and I drove over to the earth in his Land-Rover – and reckless fool that I was, asked if I could try San to ground. It was the most foolhardy thing I could suggest. The earth was surrounded by hunt supporters, all of whom owned utterly game terriers (that, today, they just happened to have left behind), and all ready to belittle any achievement and to ridicule any failure. I felt very much alone, standing there on the edge of an earth trying to enter a terrier who had reputedly jibbed and run from fox. But as I told you, San never let me down or made me look a fool in public, and he didn't now. He flew in, giving tongue like a booming drum. A scuffle, a brief period of frantic baying and the fox flashed out of the earth and away. 'Hell of a terrier that,' beamed the Master, gently flicking me with his crop (oh good, I am 'wanted' again) before he was gone.

How can anyone who has not trained a dog understand the fierce exultation that possesses and consumes the hunter when his dog, well and truly trained and entered to a quarry, gives his first successful public performance (for there is something of the ham in all of us)? Who else can know that feeling of pride? Perhaps it is the pride experienced by a Michelangelo gazing up at a creation in a Sistine chapel, or a Donne exuberant after a sermon, but I doubt it, for there is something superbly primitive in harnessing a dog to one of man's oldest pursuits, and it gives me a sensation so strong that I feel like shouting, 'Tonight I am a wolf and tonight I will howl.' Augustus boasted he found Rome built of clay and rebuilt it of marble, but I had been given a failure, a dismal drop-out, a canine catastrophe, and had produced a masterpiece of hunting from raw and damaged goods.

That night we walked the grimy backstreets of Rotherham together, my shortcomings as a teacher things of minor importance. Hope does indeed spring eternal, and a man has only to experience the tiniest degree of success to banish the misery of a lifetime of failure. A nation needs only one king, but each man must be that king. Hence the meek and the mild, trampled and torn by the rat-race of man's existence, resort to keeping rabbits, canaries or doves, for winning with them at shows gives a man the sensation of being master of all men – his red cards will be his crown, and the admiration of his fellow exhibitors his courtly worship. One great triumph is better than a lifetime of half-success. I was a poor teacher, but I had trained one hell of a good terrier.

To develop a link with any dog of this type is essential, and it is only the solitary hunter who forges such a link. Men who hunt in bands puzzle me. The incessant testing of their dogs (and selves), and the bitter rivalry that develops between terrier-owning friends, mystifies me. I had other terriers, but San I hunted alone. I would sit on the fence of a tip and watch him quarter the ground like a shaggy, ugly, miniature foxhound, indulging in insane flights of phantasy as I did so. Buddha came upon his philosophical ideas meditating under a tree. Me? Well, I gained my oblique and slightly zany views on life while watching a dog hunting   flights of phantasy are my speciality. Once, in school, I was severely thrashed for roaring with laughter when, in my mind's eye, I saw a young Picasso bowed in humiliation while his teacher came across to the student's surrealist mess and said, 'Oh no, Pablo, I must have a word in your eye!' The insane, promotion-seeking, fast-buck-chasing world could race on past. Me? I was like W. H. Davies, requiring time to just stand and stare.

77

Time enough for reverie, for reputations are made in the field, not in dreams, and San was five years old, with much time to make up. It was a winter of foxes, and by the time huntsmen began to whip hounds off pregnant vixens, San had done considerable work and won his first working certificate – a scrap of paper for a winter's hard graft. He was, to be honest, becoming rather hard, and took to damaging a few of his foxes quite badly before he persuaded them to bolt, but he received for his troubles a very bad battering from the last fox he bolted. This dog fox had lodged between two subterranean boulders and waited for the dog to squeeze between the stones before slashing him badly. Phil, a veritable cyclone with a spade, dug to him and found San still at his fox, but his face caked with mud and blood. It had been a hard dig – two hours of ripping and hacking at that cemented conglomerate men rightly call 'fox bench' which is deadly to dig through.

So winter faded into spring and spring blossomed into summer. Fox hunting had ended. Vixens took their cubs out of foetid earths into the cool comfort of growing corn and bracken, and it was no longer feasible to hunt with a terrier. I still worked rat regularly, of course, and won minor sums from men who had not heard of my dog's prowess – and, to tell the truth, came close to losing one wager against a most unlikely opponent, a mongrel Welsh terrier as quiet and retiring as my own dog, but a lightning-fast, quick-killing dog whose ability belied his docile exterior. My diary reads 'won 14–12', but it gives no indication of the titanic struggle that gave rise to that score. At one time we were 6–2 down and only narrowly defeated our opponent. Anyway, his owner paid me the £5 without too much complaint, but was foolish enough to gamble double or nothing on the next contest. Here, psychology on my part and breeding on San's part came into play. After the first contest, both dogs were badly bitten – mistrust anyone who says that their dogs rat regularly and are never bitten – and both dogs' faces swelled until they looked like bull terriers. So I decided to play next evening. Each dog's face and mouth was very tender, but we won 16–4. It takes a game dog to kill rats in number with his face very badly swollen from rat bites. This is probably why the valley 'oldies' crossed in the formidable fighting bull-terrier blood – blood that proved such a curse underground, and was so useful in a crunch.

Those were happy days, the whole summer spent hunting and chattering amiably with fellow hunters while I bathed in the reflected glory of my terrier. My escapades invariably brought shaking heads and muttered tut-tuts from fellow teaching staff, but these mattered little and they could indulge in their didactic babbling while leaving my hunting strictly alone.

At the outset of this chapter I mentioned that San had one fault or failing – or was it a mirror image of my own personal dislikes and selfishness? I must now make a confession – and for a teacher it is one hell of a confession. I dislike small children to the point of hatred. Small children or babies brought to my cottage and allowed to rampage, as small children invariably do, put me in such a fury that I am physically ill and gladly make enemies of friends who have brought them to ruin the peace of my home. My dogs are usually good-natured and accept these nuisances, stoically allowing their feet to be stepped on and their ears and tails to be tugged. I cannot accept small children and feel that people who realize my antipathy towards infants should have the good sense or manners not to bring them to my cottage. But few have this sense, and most invariably allow children to cascade from their cars and disrupt the solitude of my isolated home – though they only do it once, I hasten to add, for in addition to being a child-hater I am also extremely rude. It was for these reasons that I avoided emotional entanglements with women who had tiny children and only once made the mistake of inviting one such back to my home.

I was walking through Rotherham one Saturday that glorious summer in order to purchase goods necessary for my frugal existence during the following week, and there I met a very pretty woman who, it transpired, had once been married (and had a tiny child from the union). Against my better judgement, I started taking her out, but try as I might I could not feel anything but distaste for the child whose sticky hands were besmirching my wallpaper and furniture. He was a pleasant child – now a very intelligent young man, I believe – but I just had to face it, I dislike babies. Carol, my divorcee girl friend, took to carrying him across town to my place in some weird carry-cot affair, and the child would sleep in its box for hours at a stretch in my living room. (I am amazed at small children, whose lives consist of eating, sleeping and defecating.)

San would have nothing to do with Carol or Gareth, her child, and watched from the safety of the back of the settee – never threatening, snarling or menacing, but simply watching the small child. It was ominous, and if I had realized I might have prevented the storm from happening. One day Carol and I left the room to go into the kitchen – no great distance in a two-up, two-down cottage – leaving the baby in the living room with San. Gareth began to yell and then became silent, which I am told is the usual way with infants, but a staccato bumping made it all too apparent that something was wrong. We returned to find San had dragged the bundle containing the infant from his cot and was in process of shaking him to death – rather in the way that I had seen him kill a smallish fox. I had literally to kick him unconscious to stop him killing the child.

What reason possessed him, this cold, stoical, indifferent dog, to do this, I will never know. Perhaps he disliked children as much as I did – or could it be that he sensed my antipathy and sought to win my approval by killing the child? As I have said, I will never know. It may not have been jealousy, for I had never touched the child nor even spoken to him. Whatever the reason, it brought my relationship with Carol to a crisis and resulted in the usual 'Either him or me' speech. The choice was all too obvious. Women were easy to get, but where would I find a dog like this again?

Well, summer waxed and waned and eventually begat autumn, but the cutting of the corn and the fall of the leaves put the foxes back below ground, so away we went on the seasonal merry-go-round of fox hunting, though this year Phil and I did not see exactly eye-to-eye on certain subjects. The rift between us began when there was a knock on my front door one Saturday morning. My caller was one, Jack Anson, a noted lurcher man who had brought his 'in season' terrier bitch to be mated with my dog. His bitch was a neat, stylish little Jack Russell, and I had some qualms about putting my hideous dog to her. I needn't have worried. Not only was San a demon rat killer, he was also damned-nigh impotent and was to be eight years old before he would even look at a bitch. Returning to Jack, however, it transpired that he was not at all popular with Phil, who regarded him as a bit of an anathema, for Jack made quite a sizeable chunk of his money by selling fox pelts, bolting foxes with his terrier and killing them with his collie lurchers. Hunts consider it just a little *infra dig.* to hunt for pelts, and decree that a fox should be broken up and torn, its beautiful coat wasted.

At that time Jack was out of work – and still is, for that matter – and sold the pelts of foxes for between £2 and £4. (Prices have rocketed since, and good-quality pelts now fetch up to £15 each.) Phil hated him, for Jack had spoilt the sport on many occasions by visiting the district a day or so before and taking the foxes. This is so easily done that it was a bit unworthy of Jack, who was a very good hunter. It was enough to create bad feeling at the hunt, however, for whereas those who ride to hounds go along for the ride rather than the kill, they do need something to gallop after. That I had even allowed Jack to my house was the reason for the start of the rift between Phil and me – a rift that was to widen to a chasm when I too started hunting fox for pelts.

In many ways, I regretted breaking with Phil, but at that time £4 was good money, and as I had terriers and Jack had excellent lurchers, it was an opportunity too good to miss. Anyway, no matter what one does it offends somebody. (Bob Martin, who teaches contraception to the kids in my present school, probably lives in constant danger of an assassin from Mothercare!) Sixty years ago, Jack's lot and mine would have been different. The Yorkshire hunting fraternity was powerful then, and they would have found something to ruin us. Jack would have been thrown out of his cottage and I would have been called before the school board and dismissed. Indeed, the hunts were very powerful some seventy years ago. Men who had the temerity to shoot a fox even on their own land would wake in the morning to find scarlet-clad Kluxers had pinned a note saying 'This man shot a fox' to their gates. Times have changed, however. We were simply boycotted, and I lost a good friend in Phil.

Winter ended, and I had pelt money enough to buy a three-piece suite. Nothing elaborate. I still have it. But San was becoming a legend up north. 'Best little terrier in the north,' was the supreme compliment – a great accolade from a Yorkshireman to a mere Welshman. Summer times are a bit dead for a terrier man, and though I did hunt a few badger, I never had much desire to molest this overgrown and harmless stoat. As I hope I have demonstrated amply in an earlier chapter, his flesh is totally inedible, while his pelt is maybe worth 75p as a curio. Furthermore, he is such a fearsome fighter that the damage he can do to a terrier is frightful, can be irreparable and outweighs any pleasure obtained in hunting him. I am somewhat prejudiced in this respect since as I told I lost San's brother Dusty hunting them, and I was nearly to lose San in the same way.

It happened one Sunday afternoon when Bill Brockley invited a girl friend and me to Etwall for tea, and, of course, I took San with me. As we walked across the fields after tea, San put his nose down and began questing frantically. He struck a line and ran straight to an artificial earth that held a moderately large boar badger, driven off from the breeding earth by his sire, no doubt, for this artificial earth has held a number of in-transit boars over the years I have known Bill. In he went, and alas was followed by Bill's terriers, not one of which was on a lead, for we were not expecting a hunt. San was at the boar before I could stop it – a very dangerous business in a drainpipe, for a dog has no room to manoeuvre. San locked on to the boar and began to drag it out of the drain. Now it is quite possible for a dog to drag a badger from an earth of this type – quite easy, in fact, but not with eleven dogs wedged behind him, one of which was so frantic that she savaged San's hind legs. However, by dint of taking out the hindmost terrier we managed to get the rest out and San drew the badger.

As the badger cleared the drain, all hell broke loose with the rest of the terriers, and in the mêlée that followed the badger broke away. He bolted down a small grassy bank just as I leapt on him to take him, and I rolled with him down the precipitous sides with dogs and badger snapping at me. I tried desperately to hold him, but he made it to a lair in a near-by sand pit and I was forced to give him best.

San looked decidedly off-colour, and examination revealed ghastly lacerations. His jaws were broken, his front paw smashed to a mass of shattered bone and mangled flesh, and his throat so badly torn that I was amazed shock did not carry him off before we got him back to Bill's house. He bled profusely, and it was with great difficulty that the vet managed to stop the bleeding. It was autumn before he could walk again, let alone hunt.

How does one spotlight events in a hunting career as glorious as this dog's was? Sufficient to say that he was to become immortal in both the north and the midlands. All this in spite of a tragedy which struck him during his ninth year. We were at that time hunting a district called Hathersage, just south of Sheffield, for a vixen had come down, probably out of the Peak District, and was causing havoc in the locality. She seemed totally unafraid of dogs – something very wrong here, for foxes are terrified of domesticated dogs – and would gleefully pull boards off poultry houses to kill the terrified poultry within, heedless of the barking of chained-up farm dogs. The land hereabouts was rocky, and the earths invariably the sets of badgers, so to avoid the necessity of digging, I set swivel-type fox snares that were self-locking, preventing the escape of the fox if it once hit the wires. I took a great deal of time setting these snares, gauging height, weight and so forth, and though I caught three innocent dog foxes, the killing continued. The vixen seemed to take a delight in getting her living from around human habitation.

To this day I remain convinced that she had been taken as a cub and reared as a pet, but was turned loose when her owners realized that foxes are not bushy-tailed dogs and are very wild and intractable, for nothing else could explain her total disrespect for dogs. I nearly taught her the folly of her ways one night in January. I was lamping rabbits with a small greyhound bitch who was not particularly bright – few greyhounds are – but she was a devil of a killer, and I had to watch her with sheep for she was inclined to put in the odd nip or so when coursing through them. This particular night the vixen stepped straight into the beam and stood there, luminous saucer eyes reflecting the light from the lamp. She turned and I saw her distinctly, a fairly large, tall fox with a poor brush. My greyhound also saw her and bore down on her like the wings of death. At the very last moment, my vixen bowled over and slipped through a tiny gap in the hedge, leaving the greyhound standing there with the stupid expression all thwarted greyhounds seem to put on.

Any vixen who hangs around a district creating carnage of this nature is doomed, however, and the sands of time were running out for her. One cold afternoon, Laurie, my Sheffield-based co-hunter, came racing across to my house in his car. A shepherd had seen our vixen carrying a dead guinea-fowl to an earth, and he had had the foresight to wall her in with huge stones. We arrived at the earth early in the afternoon, and in spite of Laurie's enthusiasm, Jack and I winced. It was only a one-holed set, but the place was a labyrinth of tunnels between huge boulders – a death-trap for any terrier. Still, we knew we might never get another such chance at her, so it had to be now or never. I first put in Wanton, a great granddaughter of Cobby's Pickaxe and a truly sensible bitch to ground. A frantic barking began, punctuated with the sound of her jumping. She emerged in the evening, exhausted and her face a red ruin. I gauged that the fox must be lying up in a gap between boulders a few feet above the tunnel entrance.

The old dog sniffed Wanton's fox-smelling face and whined piteously. I slipped San and he slid carefully into the earth. Almost immediately a thunderous baying began, and also the sound of jumping, but it was to be three days before San was to emerge, dragging the dead vixen with him. He was a mass of wounds, but I was not too worried – he had been bitten up before and had recovered. The damage, however, was worse than expected. Investigation by vets revealed that the fight had damaged the optic nerve and San was totally blind. Fool that I was, I could have called him out at any stage in that dig!

At first I thought it kindness to put the old warrior to sleep, but even if hell has me, I cannot find it in my heart to kill one of my dogs. He in fact adjusted remarkably well, and ratted well enough, provided one kept one's feet still and didn't confuse him. He was also still a useful dog below ground, for sight is a minor consideration when hunting in the Stygian darkness of a deep earth, and during the next few years we hunted wildcat and coypu with him, as well as fox and the occasional badger.

Time came, however, when he no longer wanted to leave his kennel to hunt with me, and one day I found him quite dead, his lips twisted in the awful rictus of death, revealing stumps of aged teeth. Since time has begun, poets and writers have written elegies on the death of favourite dogs. Hogg, Southey, Scott and even Kipling eulogized over their pets and made their passing poetic. All a dog had to do was to sit and gaze lovingly at his master to be immortalized. I had had the best, most loyal terrier of my life, valiant unto death, game as a bantam cock and a pleasure to hunt. It is a sad reflection on me that the only elegy I could think of as I wiped tears from my face was, 'Christ, you're ugly.'

6 *First Hawk*

Predators hold a fascination for me. Nothing can keep my interest like watching a stoat hunt feeding doves, or a fox stalk a rabbit with a feline stealth, and I can feel my heart beating in accord with the hunter rather than the hunted. I was introduced to predatory birds at a very early age. Most miners in South Wales have kept racing pigeons at some time in their lives, and it seemed to be the *raison d'être* of most of the valley boys some thirty years ago. Most of the menfolk rarely left Wales, but indulged in massive escapism by sending their racing pigeons to race home from such exotic-sounding places as Saint-Malô, Nantes, Libourne or Bordeaux.

The route south holds a magic that cannot be equalled by flying similar distances into the very heart of industrial England. It was certainly a form of escapism. Perhaps sending his pigeons on races of great distances was the Welsh miner's way of saying, like Saul of Tarsus, 'But I was born free.' Many of the valley boys have an almost obsessive love for their pigeons, and will go without food to buy good-quality maple peas to feed them, waiting through the night in their lofts to 'clock in' racers who have not made it home before nightfall. When I was a lad there was a saying that there were no happily married pigeon flyers, for the preoccupation with their birds made them neglect their wives and children. It is scarcely surprising that such devotees of pigeon racing have little time for hawks and their bedfellows.

Yet hawks and falcons were quite common near my home. Long before man burrowed into the earth for coal, the Ice Age glaciers ripped large chunks out of the head of the valley, leaving the hill-sides steep and precipitous and the head of the valley almost unclimbable to anyone who was not a mountaineer. Even a baboon could not have climbed these cliff-like rock faces, and it was here

85

that the peregrines nested, giving pigeon flyers heart attacks and creating bedlam among the pigeons exercising in the late afternoon. During the Second World War, the Ministry of Defence, aware that these falcons killed carrier pigeons, declared war on the peregrine, but although a few were shot, there was little a shotgun could do to a bird coasting arrogantly at 2,000 feet. They would hang almost indolently, a black speck against the sky, and then drop like a stone among a flock of exercising racing pigeons, hitting the luckless selected victim an almighty smack, driving the bird to the ground and then breaking its neck with a sharp, 'toothed' beak.

It was during my ninth year that my interest in these birds began. It was our customary Saturday treat to sit on the stone garden walls and watch the pigeons race home from the south to lofts where excited owners rattled tins of corn to entice the birds in and stamp the race rings on the ticking pigeon clock. To the child today, who has his sound sensations provided by hi-fi, his visual experiences by television, it must seem a frightfully dull way to spend a Saturday, but to us it was the highlight of the week. It was the August holidays, warm and happy as all the Augusts of childhood seem to be, for at the age of nine, 'the sweet bird of youth' had scarcely developed down, let alone begun to discontentedly flap its wings.

Pigeons were returning from Weymouth, or perhaps Guernsey, and anxious owners stood in the doors of their lofts with eyes eagerly and worriedly watching the only entrance to our valley. Pigeon flyers have amazing eyesight, far superior to that of the average man; long before we lads could discern whether or not the bird was a pigeon rather than a chimney-dwelling jackdaw, the pigeon flyer would identify it as his blue hen carrying hope and pool money back to its loft. This particular day was an ideal day for racing, clear skies and a wind sweeping up the valley from the sea.

High above our rows of terraced houses hung a young peregrine, bored and petulant as a young princess and idle as only a predator can afford to be. Ancestors of hers had been sent in hampers to the kings of far-off London, fed on puppies during the journey. This one swung above us, making half-hearted feints at pigeons, sometimes dusting their feathers as an indifferent gesture. She flew casually above the High Street, a thoroughfare of mean terraces, damp and dark, beloved by tuberculosis germs and enjoyed by sociologists. Only an earl could own such a bird. How out of place she appeared here! Suddenly a young racebird came in across the valley, fanning its tail to brake and land in the loft, breaking away from the main batch that had towed it back from the south coast of England. My peregrine had climbed higher, and for some reason my eyes focused on her. Battle flight! And she came crashing down like a stone, the wind whistling through her feathers, hitting the pigeon maybe a hundred feet above my head. The pigeon plummeted, descending earthwards like an awkward feather duster, and hit the cobbled lane only six feet from where I sat. It was dreadfully lacerated, crop torn open and sternum smashed – a sickening sight for a young child. It was perhaps at that moment that I resolved before I left the valley I would own such a bird.

Not only peregrines exacted a toll among the pigeons. Three miles from where I lived was a patch of woodland that had somehow escaped the despoliation of timber the rest of the valley had suffered, and in these woods nested that elegant, mad-eyed, stilt-legged paranoid, the sparrowhawk. Sparrowhawks were to be my first falconry birds – no, alas, let us be truthful, my first victims, the first creatures to meet their death through me. During the weekends I literally combed those woods for the nests of sparrowhawks made of sticks and twigs and often the deserted lairs of last year's crows. I think I was ten years old when I excitedly brought home my first nest of sparrowhawks. My victims were three large females and a weedy little male. Male sparrowhawks, or muskets, are naturally puny and always difficult to rear. For myself, I was overjoyed, unaware of the tragedy that was to overtake these creatures.

It was the time of meat rationing, just after the Second World War – a lean time with scarcely enough food for people, let alone hawks. Their mother would have hunted non-stop to fill those shrieking mouths with finches, sparrows, linnets and blackbirds. I shot a few sparrows with my catapult, trapped a few mice in my breakback trap, but it was not enough to keep my nestlings alive. Their screaming became intense and then gradually weaker, and one by one they expired, the tiny, huge-eyed male first, and last of all the biggest female, who stood balancing on one leg like an emaciated stork before she too fell and died. To lose young animals and birds always induced a gloom and a giant depression in me, partly because of guilt at taking them from their mother, who would easily have fed them, in this case from those finch-filled woods, and partly through despair at being unable to stop the inevitable. I can understand the mental attitude of a bitch who, in despair, savages and eats an ailing puppy whose constant bleating has infuriated and distressed her. Likewise I find it easy to understand the loving mother of a sickly baby who suddenly turns to child battering, for I know how both must feel.

Youth, however, is resilient as a rubber ball, and when the next season came around I again procured a hatch of these diminutive hawks, and again succeeded only in killing the entire nest. No one in the valley knew anything about falconry, and my only source of books was the Ffaldau Working Men's Library that housed numerous copies of *Das Kapital*, ready to saturate the minds of future young socialists discontented with the world, but nothing to satisfy the needs of an earthy malcontent eager to keep his hawks alive and let the rest of the world take care of itself. My father at last administered one of his few paternal lectures, one eye on the clock as the hands came round to opening time, and forbade me to try to rear another nest of hawks.

It was certainly for the best. During the course of the Second World War, science, devoid of any knowledge of ecology or living together, came up with one of its deadliest blunders, and invented Aldrin and other lethal chlorinated hydrocarbons, substances that devastated not only insect pests, but also seed-eating birds and even predators to such an extent that the sparrowhawk would certainly have been extinct in Pandy had I persisted in my attempts to rear other nests.

My interest in hawks did not diminish, however. Throughout my unhappy youth to my dismal military service and on into college, I maintained my interest in avian predators, reading everything I could about them, from the totally bewildering book by Frederick II, who, though historians referred to him as *Stupor Mundi* – wonder of the world – left me a little cold, to historical novels whose writers usually researched medieval kings well enough, but the art of falconry not at all. A book, in fact, had only to contain a veiled reference to falconry for me to read it, but it was to be 1961 before I obtained a predator to train, and even he wasn't a true hawk. One's first hawk should be chosen with care, and only a lunatic takes on a fiery goshawk, or the easily ruined peregrine. It is far better to start with the phlegmatic kestrel or, as in my case, the docile buzzard. I therefore wrote to the Home Office for a permit to take a buzzard. (In those days, I still did most things by the book, as

I had hopes of promotion and even a headship; it was only later that I really kicked over the traces.) I contacted a really good falconer and ordered my buzzard.

I can still feel the excitement of racing down to the railway station to collect the large cardboard box that smelled of soap and bird manure and contained my bird. I half-expected to find him a dominant primordial creature, with a pulsating fury radiating from him. In this I was disappointed – bitterly disappointed. Jim had taken my buzzard young, and it was so tame that within ten minutes of being released from its soapbox he was scuttling around the room like a feathered crab shrieking for food. Pelaw, as I called him, was a superb example of what psychologists call malimprinting and falconers call a 'screamer'. Taken from his nest at an impressionable age, he would for ever after regard Jim or a substitute human as his parent, the screaming which persisted well into adulthood simply being an indication that it wished to be acknowledged or, better still, fed.

Anyway, I set to and fitted him with jesses, straps of leather attached to his legs, so that I could carry him wherever I wished. They were totally superfluous, for he would follow me wherever I went, bleating loudly for food and attention. I went through the basic motions of training, which consist of simply calling the bird to the fist. I even attached a length of twine, or 'creance' as they call it in falconry parlance, but as soon as I moved away from the bird he flew to me instantly, perching on my shoulders and head if I could not offer my fist as a perch. He was charming, a delightful pet, but not at all what I required.

With basic training completed, however, I went about trying to fly him at quarry. I starved him for two days to the point where he aroused my sympathy by his 'upside-down head' glances and his fearful, perpetual bleating, but after that interval I deemed him ready. My first bid at entering him to quarry proved disastrous as a cry from a rather silly girl friend, emitted at the moment of impact of talon on rat, deterred him from further attempts at rat hunting. Like the wee cooper of Fife's wife, he was totally useless, but unlike the said woman, he could not be beaten into submission. Submissive he already was – far too submissive to be of any use as a hunting bird – so reluctantly I resolved to 'hack him back', as they say in the baffling, dated parlance of falconry, meaning gradually turn him loose, allowing him to fend for himself. It had to be a gradual process as he was totally incapable of looking after himself, and far too unsuspecting of people to survive in a hostile world. T. H. White, in his masterpiece *The Goshawk*, states that after two or three days of liberty a hawk will be as wild as when he was first taken, but I had grave doubts in the case of my silly buzzard. I could not see any chance of him becoming in any way wild, and I knew he could hardly survive long in a world antipathetic to predators.

Hack him back, though, I must, for my boast is that I am a hunter, and thus loth to keep any animal as just a pet, no matter how lovable and enchanting. So I would return him to his natural world after I had allowed him to gain experience of its dangers. I took off his restricting and unnecessary jesses, and placed him on the gatepost near my house. As I walked away he gave a plaintive bleat that nearly undermined my determination to free him, but I had resolved to do so and must not weaken now. Two hours later he was still on my gatepost, watching eagerly for any movement of the curtains. The damned bird had decided not to be hacked back, and as I approached him he flew to my hand for the meat he knew I would give him. I left him out all night, and dawn found him in a beech tree opposite the house. If he had shut up he would have been unnoticed, but he began that inane, pitiful bleating as soon as he saw me. I fed him and threw him off again, and he glided back to his beech tree. I had an awful feeling that I was losing the battle. That afternoon some hunters came to see if I would ferret a barn for a colony of rats which had taken up residence in a grain store and was causing some trouble. I boxed up my ferrets, put the terriers in the boot, but I had to practically beat Pelaw off as he hustled across for food and attention.

He was still there when the van returned, greeting our arrival with his irritating, imbecilic squealing and the shuffling of his stubby feet at the excitement of being in proximity to someone who would feed him. I took four or five dead rats out of the sack to feed to the ferrets, and as an afterthought flung a small one down at the foot of Pelaw's gatepost. Pelaw stretched his neck to watch and, finally convinced that it was not a trick or a joke on my part, alighted on the carcass, footing it cautiously and pecking and prodding the reddened entrails with his beak. Next morning, Pelaw was still there but the rat was gone, head, fur, tail, the lot, and few creatures will eat a rat's tail. At first I thought a fox or a badger from the near-by set had taken it, but a glance at Pelaw's bulging crop convinced me of where the rat had gone.

Birds of prey are tamed by their food being withheld, said the old falconry books. A hungry hawk is a tame hawk, but my cardboard cut-out bird still greeted me with screams and friendship in spite of his bloated crop. I ignored him and walked down the muddy lane to work. A rabbit had been killed by a car – and as I hate waste and the meat was fresh, I flung it beneath the hedge so I could retrieve it on my return from school. In my free period I wrote two letters to Germany to try and obtain a real hawk, but I still perhaps cherished a sort of forlorn hope that Pelaw would improve and become a raging cyclone of feather and talon. Some people have had success in training buzzards for falconry, and the American red-tailed hawk is simply an aggressive, dynamic buzzard, but Pelaw – well, that was another matter.

I returned home, picked up the rabbit from its hiding place under the hedge and noticed the head was crushed, revealing long, sharp, incisors. It is amazing that a ferret will face a creature armed like a rabbit, and it must be a game ferret that will stay to a doe adamant that it will not bolt. I walked up the muddy footpath to the cottage, playing hop-scotch across the junction gateway churned to a quagmire by cows. Pelaw began to bleat long before I came into view. It is said that if you see a hawk, it has been watching you for some time. The senses of a hawk, its sight and hearing, that is, are amazingly developed, and only the sense of smell is of a very low level in birds of prey. Pelaw began to squeal loudly as soon as he saw me, and like some huge avian moth, he floated down the lane towards me, sounding his plaintive 'Hello mum' cry. Perhaps he had seen only me at first, but within twenty or thirty yards from me he noticed the rabbit. His wing-beat quickened until he was flying quite fast – fast, that is, for a buzzard, who, being a carrion eater, isn't in any hurry to be going anywhere. He struck the rabbit carcass with a thwack and hung on like a limpet with his puny little claws, screaming now in excitement and indignation at my not allowing him to dine there and then. He hung on until we reached the gateway and I threw down the carcass near the gatepost.

Pelaw attacked it with relish, ripping off slivers of meat and pieces of fur and gulping them down. Fur is fairly essential to the diet of a hawk or falcon, though not because it is digested. It is regurgitated in the form of a pellet, together with any bones or detritus that the stomach juices have failed to dissolve. It is said by old falconry books that a hawk denied such fur, known in the trade as 'casting', will quickly go off colour. Likewise stones are ingested, only to be spewed up covered in a sticky oil. These stones, known as 'wrangle', are about the size of a soya bean in the case of a buzzard and act as a type of conditioner. Birds are said to fly with greater venom at quarry after they have disgorged their stones.

Not that this concerned Pelaw. Mind you, he wasn't going to fly at anything with or without venom, but he was able to produce interesting pellets in abundance, and soon every infant school in the district had a rather nasty little bundle labelled 'Buzzard pellet' on the nature table. ('Don't touch them, darlings, the fur and bone content is rat.') Infant-school parents are decidedly kinky about nature tables, and mums and dads who will not even allow their brats to talk to kids with runny noses are usually enthusiastic about them handling buzzard pellets and minute black blobs labelled 'Mole droppings' or such-like. In fact, animal faeces seem to fascinate the upper class. King Pellinore, the celibate, eccentric knight of T. H. White's *The Sword in the Stone*, spent his entire life chasing the questing beast and collecting its fewmets, which is why, incidentally, he remained celibate – but I digress.

That night I fed the stock and must have been sloppy about locking my ferret cage – fatal, for a creature like a ferret will, unlike the biblical man of property, easily crawl through the eye of a needle, and if he can, drag a dead hen after him. Ferrets who get loose always make straight for the nearest hen-house, and morning will find them lying snugly and happily in the remains of some unfortunate fowl that has been neatly bitten through the brain and eaten while still fluttering. This ferret was an exception, however, and I was awakened at dawn by Pelaw's frantic screams. I raced out in pyjamas, noticing the ferret cage door was ajar and expecting the worst. Pelaw was dancing with rage and screaming frantically at the ferret, who was tearing with a ferocity known only to ferrets at the half-eaten rabbit four feet below Pelaw's talons.

There was something odd about the bird's behaviour – a sort of anger that was not quite him. His stubby claws drew blood from my hands as I picked him up, and he issued screams and raging threats at the ferret munching happily at the rabbit. I had a sudden feeling that Pelaw was considering the prospect of attacking the ferret and was stamping around to pluck up courage to engage in battle in the same way that a Red Indian goes into a war dance before attacking the cavalry. Could this be the same bird who, hungry as he was, would do little more than put in a half-hearted putt at a mouse-sized baby rat? I had an idea that he was ready to leave me, and my hunch proved correct. Next day when I walked up the lane to home I noticed that Pelaw did not greet me with his usual screaming. He was huddled up on the gate, his crop distended like an over-fed broody hen's. Below him on the grass lay a half-eaten doe rat, head and shoulder completely demolished and little of the viscera left. Pelaw belched happily, but as I stood up to stroke him, he edged away petulantly. Next day he was gone for good. He had finally served his apprenticeship and was off into the big, wide and, as it transpired, hostile world.

I have, I am told, an annoying habit of leaving a story half-finished, of never really completing a tale properly. I will try to do better in the case of Pelaw. What became of him? Well, as it happens, I had no idea for fifteen years, and it was only two months before I sat down to write this chapter that I learned what his fate had been. He must have found the harsh 1962–63 winter fairly easy, living on dead or dying rabbits and birds that the winter had polished off, or on sick kale-filled pigeons too weak to fly, but I never really knew. My holding went bankrupt during that spring, and this was the point when I left the country for a time.

Recently, however, I visited a school teacher who taught with me during those frigid days of the Big Winter. I suddenly felt very old, and I set to thinking of the wild days I spent in the district, so wild, in fact, that my headmaster's reference must have read like a committal notice to a lunatic asylum. The subject of my buzzard came up in our conversation. During the spring, he remarked, two workmen killed a buzzard which they alleged had attacked them. Poor, silly Pelaw therefore probably failed to make a kill that day and flew across to the men to be fed. He trusted everyone – at his peril, it seems. My friend finished his tale and put down his sherry glass, his once-young face now lined. I became suddenly aware that unless I was like Peter Pan, I too must look as old. Just as my buzzard, the sweet bird of youth, had long since flown.

7 Climber

Damn it, I hate to admit that I failed with any dog, but I did with Climber. Not that she was a coward or a non-hunter, nor was I an amateur trainer by the time she was born, but whatever the reason we just didn't 'hit it off', and eventually it became clear that, just like the Sheriff of Tombstone says in hammy Westerns, 'There ain't no room in this town for both of us, and one of us has to go' – and heck, it was my property, so it had to be her. Yes, honest to goodness, I failed with Climber and burned a candle in thanks on the day Malcolm Haddock came to take her off with him. It was all so long ago, but I can still remember those dreadful, tumultuous days as if they were yesterday.

She had a heritage of oddness – I think there is such a word. Wen, her mother – her name means 'white' in Welsh – had been far from a model terrier, but for entirely different reasons. Wen was a result of a half-brother, half-sister mating, both parents being as gutsy a pair as ever drew breath – and intelligent, too, in spite of the fact that her mother died after a bad mauling from a badger – two badgers, actually, for she became trapped between a boar and a sow. The vet had stitched her up and set her bones, lamenting that it was like putting together a flesh jigsaw puzzle, but in spite of his excellent surgery she died four days later from loss of blood and shock. Wen's sire was a killer – and that was the understatement of understatements. I had sent him to hunt service to get a working certificate, but he had proved so hard that the huntsman signed his working certificate merely to get rid of him. He was lethal with fox, rushing in for a 'catch' hold and then throttling his victim, as does a Fell terrier. He was also just a little foolhardy with badger, a rather fatal mistake often as not, for the saying, 'There are many old badger dogs, and many bold badger dogs, but there are no old bold badger dogs,' is true.

Both sire and dam were grandchildren of John Cobby's Pickaxe, a dog who did such outstanding service with the South-West Wiltshire hunt and as good and sensible a terrier as ever drew breath. So I mated the pair together in the hopes of producing a replica of old Pickaxe, but the progeny of the union, two bitches and a dog, was very variable. One bitch, called Ping by the daughter of a woman friend, was the spitting image of her illustrious great-grandfather: bold, flashy and an inveterate hunter. She took to rat hunting before her permanent teeth had even broken through the gums, and by seven months old she was well and truly wed to the sport. By a year old she had entered well to fox and gained her working certificate by the age of fifteen months – and she really did earn her award in a season when tired foxes run to ground at the end of a hunt proved the rule rather than the exception. I have seen quite a few working certificates signed by huntsmen for dogs that yapped a few times at foxes and then came out, but Ping earned hers in one of the hardest seasons in my experience.

Her brother was a somewhat slower starter – a jolly, happy dog, slow to anger, loathe to fight, but equipped with a superb nose, a powerful jaw and an amazing agility when rat hunting. At that time I hunted rat four times a week, and both dog and bitch were well and truly wed to them by the time they were ten months old. Which brings us to Wen. She was damned nigh a replica of Ping and both were dead ringers of Cobby's type of dog. I had to stare quite hard at Wen and Ping to tell them apart – in the kennels, that is. On the hunting field, my God, they were as different as chalk is from cheese. Even when not compared to her illustrious sister, Wen could only be described as a flop. Rats fascinated her, she could sit and watch them for hours (sorry, Jerome K. Jerome). She had no interest in killing them or even chasing them, but my, they really did fascinate her! Her tail would wag frantically in appreciation of both her brother's and sister's deeds, but she never sought to emulate them.

At one time I thought Wen could have been a plant or changeling introduced into my team by the League Against Cruel Sports. Her stupidity was amazing. One day I ran her through a dry drain in Congleton merely as a training exercise. She ambled in casually and ambled out equally casually some twenty yards away. I was about to put her back on her lead and move on when I noticed my rough-coated terrier San going frantic, pulling at his leash and pawing the entrance to the earth. He was perhaps ten years old at the time, and despite being blinded had never false marked, so I was a little mystified at his attitude. He was beside himself, almost squealing with excitement. Sometimes dogs develop intense jealousy at another terrier going to ground, but he was such an old soldier that I could not believe this of him.

I put Wen back on the lead and slipped the old dog. He rocketed into the drain, baying frantically. A big dog fox, tail in a gale, exploded from the end of the twelve-inch drain, hotly pursued by my veteran; Wenny wagging her tail in appreciation. How on earth she managed to pass that fox in a twelve-inch drain is still a mystery to this day, but somehow she managed to do it! The fox was so ready to bolt that she would have needed only to brush against him to bolt him. Contrary to what may be written in north country novels written by pseudo-hunters who have never seen a fox, Reynard wants no trouble and, confronted by a dog, seems enthusiastic to leave an earth rather than make a fight of it – if he's fresh and not aware of the danger above ground, that is. Why this fox did not bolt when Wenny squeezed past him is an unsolved mystery.

I was considering getting rid of my genial clown when the penny dropped, and dropped suddenly. She was about fifteen months old when, in despair, or to make up the number, I took her ratting with some real terriers. She suddenly came to life and slew twelve in a time that would have made Billy, the noted dog of the Victorian rat pits who, according to Henry Mayhew, once killed a thousand rats at the rate of one every three seconds, worry about his reputation. Next she entered to fox without a great deal of encouragement, and a few days later went to badger. From then on she went from strength to strength. There is a lot to be said for late entering, for the dog has had time to mature before being pitted against heavy game, and although I believe that Wenny would have liked to have been noted in the *Guinness Book of Records* for dotage entering, she certainly became a useful hunting dog. She had a year's hunt service to her credit by the time she was three, and had seen considerable service bolting for lurchers before I decided to breed from her.

I had already sorted out her mate – her great-nephew, in fact, out of a daughter of her brother, and sired by Charlie Lewis's Micky, a grand show dog and a first-class worker. Rupe, as the sire was to be called, was to become one of the noted sires of ten-inch bolting dogs, but Wenny was his first mate. He was a damned good rat killer, but at the time of mating had never been tried to fox or badger, so why I decided to use him was a bit of a puzzle. I could have used maybe fifty suitable sires, but for some reason I chose this nine-month-old male. What a fortuitous choice it turned out to be.

After much fuss and bother, Rupe mated her, and some fifty-eight days later she produced a litter of seven puppies, so uniform that it would have been hard to fault them. Wen had a hell of a time rearing them, and I spent many hours snaring and lamping rabbits to feed the growing litter, for they were loath to feed after Wen's milk ran out, as it did on the fifteenth day after whelping. A lady friend – very respectable, who dropped me like a red-hot coal when she found out my true nature – was alarmed at my hunting late at night. 'Aren't you afraid that someone nasty is lurking out there in the darkness?' she said. Four weeks later she realized that the nastiest thing lurking out there was me, and left!

The litter grew slowly to begin with, for, being denied their mother's milk, they became pot-bellied with huge heads and bulging eyes. But at five weeks of age they were eating well, taking flesh, fur and bone from the rabbit carcasses I hammered to pulp with a mallet. At five weeks old I put a still-born goat (whole) in with them and that seemed to turn the tide. Lusty strong puppies now grew out of the pitiful runts of four weeks of age. When, if ever, will I breed a litter of puppies like those again?

Janey, one of the first to leave the box, went to the United States, where she is the old lady of a fashionable hunt kennel in New England.

Bobby (no, I didn't name either of the first two) went to Ray Close, a scientist drop-out friend who took more fox with Bobby and his two deerhound/greyhound lurchers than any two hunts in Britain.

Penny was sold to an old woman in Alrewas, as a pet, not a worker, but she proved so destructive and wilful that the old lady phoned the Meynell Hunt kennels and Penny finished up with Barry Dainty, who became terrier man for the Warwick Hunt at Kineton. And a remarkable bitch she proved to be, working a full season with hounds, but then sadly killed in a kennel fight. I believe Cliff Morgan of Kineton has a puppy from her still alive.

Tucker, a rather small dog, went to Keith Chalmers, a deer-stalker in Scotland. Keith had made deerstalker the hard way, for he began his career as a dentist. I never cared much for this puppy as he was a sloppy and sycophantic dog, but Keith took a very impressive head of fox and wildcat with him, so he served him well enough.

Coin, a hard-coated bitch, had a very chequered career. I sold her to a woman from Birmingham who, it transpired, was thoroughly neurotic and attention-demanding, and when her husband left her (or rather escaped) she began the customary mental trauma and took it out on the puppy and her nauseating child. To cut a long story short, Mummy went scatty, child became maladjusted, and dog savaged child. So I repaid the money and gave the bitch to Jim French, the Meynell terrier man. She was to serve him well in the Meynell, Atherstone, Hampshire and Cotswold Hunts, and I believe she is still alive today. Coin was as game a dog as I have ever seen, and in the right hands she was a treasure.

Q, a large puppy, went to a friend who returned her to me some six months later as he had matrimonial troubles. Meanwhile that left me with the choice of the litter, namely Climber – and it was the wrong choice as it transpired.

I called her Climber for at ten weeks old she could climb a five-foot wire partition and invade other pens. It was damned nigh impossible to keep her in, and though she had an endearing disposition (what ten-week-old puppy hasn't?), her escapology caused me concern. I had seven fiery stud dogs at that time, any one of which could have been spiteful enough to kill a puppy of her age. In short, she was a constant worry to me. So much for the name; now for the real problems.

At that time I had taken on the task of training three Border terrier puppies, sired by Roger Clements's Hanley Castle Russ, a young show-bred Lakeland called Rusty, and two Jack Russell terrier puppies, one of which was Climber. First task – livestock breaking; and the first livestock to steady them to – ferrets. This is very easy with puppies (though very much more difficult with adult dogs), since a good strong hob ferret, preferably a mean liner, will badly frighten most puppies. Thus I would allow the eight-week-old puppies to walk in the ferret enclosure while I cleaned out the ferret cages and gave the occupants a chance to scamper around. An enthusiastic or exuberant puppy is taught, and taught quickly, that a nip from a ferret is a bit disconcerting. I have only had one failure using this method – and here it comes.

The puppies were about fourteen weeks old at the time, Climber being about two weeks younger than the rest, and all would drink from the same bowl as the ferrets – and at the same time, I may add. I was half-way through mucking out my ferrets when the phone rang. I left the compound to answer it, but it was merely a girl friend called Angela, whose claim to fame was that she had a job advertising aftershave on TV (which she must have found a refreshing change after my constant ferrety scent). She kept me talking for maybe ten minutes before I could return to my ferret compound. A strange smell greeted me as I walked down the path. Ferrets are normally more than just a bit pungent at the best of times, but when upset their stench is frightful. The compound really stank. I found the three Borders and the Lakeland cowering under the hutches, the Russell bitch gazing in wonder from another corner and Climber locked in combat with my liner hob, who was certainly having the best of the battle. She was streaming with blood from a mass of puncture holes and he was in such a fury that his anal glands had exploded, releasing the ghastly-smelling fluid. Two dead jills lay under the cages. Climber was more than half-dead by the time I got her to the vet, but recovered after a massive antibiotic injection.

She was, however, well and truly on the way to becoming a big problem with ferrets. I would take her on a lead to the cages and yank her lead to pull her off her feet every time she lunged at the ferrets, but it did little good. After a few moments of this training she tended to ignore the ferret, but each time my back was turned she would be hell-bent on killing one. I tried everything, from thrashing her savagely – so savagely, in fact, that I felt ashamed of myself – to getting the latest researches on how Professor Eysenk was trying to break criminals of crimes of violence. I read Anthony Burgess's *The Clockwork Orange*, the hero of which, Alex, so resembled Climber that I wondered whether some form of drug injection might break the damned lunatic of ferret killing. Failure one: I could not break her to ferret.

Cat breaking was less of a problem, as I owned a Siamese female so fierce that she could put an attacking Hydra to flight. I introduced Climber to her when the bitch was ten weeks old. Pi spat at her, hurled out a claw-filled paw, and Climber's tail went between her legs. So far so good, and at ten weeks old Climber was well and truly broken to cat. At six months old, however, Climber came on an old tom-cat lying up and living rough on the Common Grove. He must have been asleep and Climber probably awakened him. He didn't wait for trouble and attacked, bowling her over in the fury of the onslaught.

I expected her to run for home, and for four or five yards she did; but suddenly the smooth silky fur stood on end, and looking twice her normal size she rounded on the tom-cat, screaming like a banshee. It was a fearsome fight: a fully grown tom-cat and a six-month-old puppy rolling in the undergrowth, ripping and tearing at each other. I had to stop them – dogs are so easily blinded or disembowelled by the claw-filled hind paws of a cat – but by now they had rolled under the brambles, neither prepared to give an inch. I beat my way through, feeling just a little like Percival Cresare who was killed by a cat, and after much clubbing retrieved the snarling, roaring Climber, who, in her fury at being pulled off her prey, savaged my hand quite badly. It was an understandable mistake – her dander was up and to her my hands were merely extensions of the cat. Be that as it may, she had still inflicted a deep puncture and as soon as we got back I dropped her in the run to allow me to boil some salt water to disinfect the wounds.

I was awakened from my pain-induced trance by a terrible caterwauling from outside. Caterwauling was right. Climber had cornered Pi against the bathroom waste pipe and was really tearing into the startled Siamese, who up until then regarded every dog as just one of the family. I climbed out of the window and had to literally kick Climber off the cat. I was a little reluctant to chance my hands again, for there was a light of battle in her eyes that bespoke of her being quite simply 'nuts', the sight of any living creature having the same effect that the rustle of a whore's petticoat had on Jack the Ripper. Stage two had also ended in failure. I had failed to break her to cats. I gave her some frightful thrashings for cat worrying, but after her sheepish look vanished she was at them again, ever ready for battle.

Ah well, at least she was broken to poultry and had run with my Indian game-cock since a baby. The gaudy cocks and stately laced-feathered hens put her in her place from six weeks old, and she now totally ignored them. It is essential for me to break dogs to poultry at an early age since, as an addicted rat hunter, I spend most of my time chasing rats around poultry farms where hens and rats live in a somewhat uneasy partnership. So I took Climber ratting, and it was here that Climber scored her first success. She was superb. Unlike her blockhead mother, Climber killed her first rat when only six months old, and polished off another six before the end of the evening. Not once did she even look at a hen. At least she could now be of some use as she was rock-steady with poultry, even killing rats between the legs of the startled fowl. Rock-steady? Well . . . maybe not quite.

I took her down my run one Saturday morning to collect the eggs from the glamorous hens and their guardian cock-bird. Climber walked obediently at heel. Something – I don't know what – made me turn. My handsome cock-bird was fluttering strangely – a sort of dervish-like dance, totally foreign to such a race of phlegmatic fowl. At first I thought he was experiencing a heart attack, for I was inclined to be a little too liberal with poultry feed and over-fed fowl are susceptible to cardiac disorders. As I neared him I realized the cause for his insane gyrations. On the grass lay his still blinking head! Climber had beheaded him with one snap as he passed un-suspectingly in front of her to get the grain.

I went berserk – shouting, lashing, throwing everything and anything at the dog, who ducked and dodged, killing the game-hens as she avoided the mass of bric-à-brac I hurled at her. Eventually, I kennelled her quickly, and walked away to prevent myself from killing her on the spot. It was damned nigh the last straw that not only broke the camel's back but also deprived me of cheap eggs to rear puppies. I was exasperated. She was, and I still believe this, undoubtedly a psychopath who would resist any form of training and conditioning and would remain calm only to erupt into furious slaying sessions as soon as my back was turned. Just as I experience great elation when successfully training a dog, I also experience terrible depression at bad failures – and I was by now very depressed. I plotted horrid deaths for her – deaths so sinister that it would have made Torquemada turn pale with envy.

It had been a wet summer and the rabbit population was increasing. So also were the foxes. James Brockley of Etwall phoned me one day and asked if I could get him a large number of fox cubs. At first I refused as I believed they were for research, and most hunters find vivisection offensive, but it transpired that some lunatic American film had shown an endearing fox cub growing up with a family who had skunks, porcupines, bobcats, rattlesnakes and a few other 'critters' that nearly every Walt Disney family seem to regard as essential in the way of mod cons as an inside 'loo'. So the world had gone decidedly daft about fox cubs. James had a

101

contract with a pet shop or something like that, but he has the sort of mind that finds it quite easy to sell a half-decayed dinosaur, so I suppose cubs weren't all that difficult to dispose of. So unhappily, but ever motivated by the thought of reward, I found myself digging and netting fox cubs galore – and boy, do I mean galore. Some four weeks and fifty-two fox cubs later, James broke the bad news: the market in fox cubs had suddenly collapsed. People had forgotten the film and the world had become indifferent to the charm of fox cubs.

I was desperate. I considered writing to the BBC begging for the film to be shown again and signing my name Jennifer, aged nine, but thought better of it. Anyway, I was stuck with my catch: fifty-two fox cubs with a strong feral smell and an appetite to remember. Not only did fifty-two fox cubs eat me out of house and home and wail piteously at night for the freedom I had reluctantly taken from them, but they also carried a pernicious form of mange mite called *Sarcoptes communis.* Furthermore, most of my terriers had seen hunt service at various fox-hunts and the scent and sound of fifty-two cubs proved alluring – alluring to such an extent that the terriers kept up a round-the-clock barking that drove me and my neighbours damned nigh mad. Add to these misfortunes the fact that I broke out in the most itching bout of scabies (due to the mange) and had to be excluded from school, and the reader will have just some idea of the troubles I experienced.

I did the only sensible thing any man could have done. I made a wax image of James Brockley, spiked it liberally with pins (it didn't work – he phoned me yesterday) and turned the whole pungent little horde loose in a district denuded of foxes through over-hunting. I shall refrain from saying where, as they caused such havoc that farmers paid me to exterminate them. Did I say I turned them all loose? Well, it's not quite true. I kept one – a beautiful silver vixen with as lovely a pelt as ever graced the neck of Jean Harlow. I had always regarded silver foxes as escaped American imports, but this one had come out of a litter of reds, so I was keen to keep her and watch her grow.

Summer suddenly became dry, and just before the corn reached a state of ripeness that can only be detected by a farmer's teeth or by some expensive and delicate equipment made only in Sweden, I received a message from Marshalls, an arable farmer ten miles distant, saying that badgers had rolled an acre of corn flat and would

I come and rid the farm of them? I have never been really keen on killing badgers as the damage done by them is vastly over-rated, but I had a market for a breeding pair from a naturalist in Market Harborough, a man who had until then never seen a badger, but who months later wrote a book about them – a common enough type of 'expert' these days. So off I went to dig my badgers, my steps motivated by the £15 my naturalist client had promised to pay. I took Wenny, my old dog San, and, as an afterthought, the slightly potty Climber. She was a year old by now, and I was certain that not only was she ready for badger, but she would have pulled down Godzilla as he happily ravaged a cardboard Tokyo.

To my total astonishment she refused even to look at badger, even when she watched Mum indulging in an awesome battle with the boar. I was utterly baffled. She didn't even attempt her usual treacherous lunge at the badgers as we 'bagged' them and hung the sack from the rack in the van. (Badgers will dig out if placed on the floor of a van.) I just couldn't understand her, and returned home leaving Jack Anson to deliver the badgers in Market Harborough. (Jack never did pay me my share of the money.) So home I went to kennel Wenny and San and put Climber in her pen by herself – for she irritated my old dog until he thrashed her. Well, I must have been a bit slap-happy about kennelling her or fastening the catches of her pen, for a few minutes later I found her screaming with rage and killing my silver fox cub that she had pulled from its cage. This was it – the last straw – *finis*. With cold fury I kennelled her and dialled Philip Clarke, a shooting man from Kenilworth. With icy precision, laced with rage, I said, 'Come over and shoot this little bastard will you, Phil? I can't take any more of her.' Climber was now well and truly under a death sentence as Phil revved up his Land-Rover and headed for Lichfield.

There's nowt so strange as folk, unless, of course, it be fate, and fate suddenly spared Climber from her well-deserved dose of number five shot. I had barely put down the phone when there was a knock at the front door. A bearded Malcolm Haddock introduced himself. He had recently taken up employment at the Meynell Hunt and had had two or three terriers knocked about a bit. He requested that I let him have a young bitch to start – and instantly I saw a way of unloading my little psychopath awaiting her executioner. Brian Forsyth of the Warwick Hunt once described her antics in his usual superb way as, 'Not quite what is required in a terrier.' Moses

Smith, my gipsy friend, not quite so poetically called her, 'Useless as a tit on a boar.' But here was a chance to get rid of her for good, and maybe even help Malcolm a little – though I confess that that thought was not uppermost in my mind. He boxed her up and, amid snorts from his ancient Mini van and sighs of relief from me, departed, leaving poor Phil to find something else to shoot. What a fortuitous union it proved to be. My total and complete failure became Malcolm's right hand. Just as Buck in Jack London's *Call of the Wild* had been a bit of a handful with everyone until he was adopted by John Thornton, so did my little psychopath adapt to Malcolm. They became a superb partnership, and though she never really lost her dread of badgers, she became one of the best fox dogs I have ever seen. Her personality may have clashed with mine but it blended with Malcolm's.

Malcolm must have had Climber for three seasons, and no hunt terrier could have worked harder. Some weeks she worked five days with the hounds, though once Malcolm came to know the district, his earth-stopping was so thorough that few foxes went to ground. Barry Dainty, then kennel man with the Meynell, tells of tremendous digs where Climber stayed eight and ten hours to a fox. She developed with Malcolm that *sympatico* relationship so essential in a working partnership but so rarely found in people today. The bitch seemed to know exactly what Malcolm wanted, whether it was a fox bolted or one bottled up so that it could be dug. During the first summer at the Meynell she came in season, and as part of our agreement Malcolm returned her to me to mate to her half-brother – who was also her distant cousin, as my strain was very inbred by now. She stood for mating, conceived and promptly set about slaying cats and poultry with the same enthusiasm she had displayed before – and was soon on her way back to Sudbury. Funnily enough, though she mated properly, she bred only one puppy in her entire life and refused to come in season again – a good job too, as I didn't want her back.

All good things come to an end, however, and during the summer following her third season at the Meynell, a very distressed Malcolm phoned to say that Climber had developed a strangulated gut and died the same night. He felt the loss more deeply than I did, for not only had she proved a loyal and hardworking companion, but she was living proof that Malcolm was a better terrier man than I was. I have always thought that Climber was a Nanga Pabat, a Bucephalus, a Gordian knot to be climbed, ridden and unravelled by the right sort of person, and I was clearly not of this mould. A sad ending. Well, not really – for her one puppy turned out to be Dune, my most famous sire and the grandfather of all my present pack.

8 *Kitchen Hawk*

After Pelaw, it was to be several years before I actually owned a hawk that would fly quarry, and those intervening years were so hard and frugal that I had scarcely enough to keep my terriers and lurchers let alone to afford another predator in my already over-stocked entourage. Once I did drop lucky and obtained a commission to translate a medieval grimoire from its bastard Latin, and with £100 burning in my pocket, I made an attempt, albeit a half-hearted one, to obtain a hawk. One of the most famous hawk-trappers in the world was, at that time, the fabulous, almost mythical Mohammed Din, a descendant of the hordes of Ghengis Khan, but now in somewhat reduced circumstances and living in 4 Rue Prem Gali (off Railway Street), Lahore, Pakistan. What an address: a scene from the *Arabian Nights* put to the sword by the words 'off Railway Street', but what's in a name, or, for that matter, an address? So I wrote to the said gentleman to inquire as to whether he could supply me with a goshawk.

At that time Mohammed Din was noted for two unique features. First, for his hawk bells, which were made from an alloy of copper so impregnated with dross that the formulas could not be duplicated and which were unequalled in the world for their crafts-manship, and secondly, for his incredible letters of reply. I never go around to buying bells directly from him, but I can vouch for his strange answering letters. To this day I still believe that the letter could have been written by someone trying to impersonate Peter Sellers' all-purpose Indian/Pakistani. It began:

Dear Sir,
  Thank you for your letter. I have a large fine strong female goshawk – Shabbuz (a very large and game goshawk) good in

feather and ideal for all game [my heart leaped up] unfortunately it is sold.'

It just had to be Peter Sellers. So, discouraged, I forgot trying to get a goshawk until three years later, when by the merest chance I came on one.

I was invited to a party by a friend who belonged to the essentially esoteric society called Mensa – in my view, a somewhat pretentious organization made up of people with I.Q.'s above 140 who appear to join the said organization through chronic (and acute) boredom and to spend their time discussing how intelligent they are. I had been invited along as the balancing ingredient to the party, a sort of earthy lunatic who could be relied on to drop a few clangers, make a fool of himself and bring just a hint of the countryside (and perhaps an odour of pig manure) into the urban sophistication. I felt a little like the court clown to make a fool of himself at medieval banquets. Anyway, the chance of a free meal and drinks lured me in.

It was a deadly evening and I desperately sought company who were not discussing something wildly esoteric and, of course, the inevitable I.Q. I slunk into a corner feeling vaguely trapped, and ventured out only to fill my glass from time to time. (Verily, I am the arch party-spoiler.) It was only after three or four minutes that I realized my sanctuary held another fugitive from the academic flood milling about us.

'Not really my scene,' I murmured apologetically, almost to myself.

'Mine neither,' was his reply, and from that moment onwards we became firm friends.

It turned out that he was a lecturer who taught the myriad tongues spoken along the shores of the Baltic, all of which sound like a vandal let loose with a rasp, and he also just happened to let drop that he was importing four goshawks from Finland. Yes, he had two to spare, and he would let me have one for the price of the carriage – £11, if I remember correctly. I am usually against impulse buying, particularly in the case of livestock, but this was an offer unlikely to be repeated, so I nearly snatched off his hand in clinching the deal.

The next week was a hive of activity. I set to work building what was, in falconry parlance, termed a 'mews' – in my case, a

blacked-out spare bedroom which had been divested of furniture.
Here I put in a padded perch to accommodate the bird. Then I
bought a large piece of fairly strong leather, cut out jesses, and
acquired a very long piece of thick but strong nylon fishing line for
a creance. The *tout ensemble* was made complete by a very long
dog lead which could be used as a leash. Few goshawks are
hooded, as are falcons, for a hawk must be carried amid the bustle
of the day, not shielded from life like a blinkered horse. Furthermore, I had once tried to hood a friend's peregrine and had come
dangerously unstuck as it bobbed and lunged to escape my blind-
fold. No, I would train my goshawk without such hoods, and train
him in the end I did, though there was to be many a slip 'twixt
obtaining and training.

To practice falconry one needs to turn back the clock five
hundred years or so to understand the quaint and out-moded
parlance of the falconer. The bird I was to be given was an 'eyass'
or nestling as opposed to the 'haggard' or wild-caught bird. The
female I was to obtain was one third again as large as the male or
'tiercel' hawk, and thus capable of taking large quarry, though by
no means as nimble and aerodynamic as the smaller male bird.

The prioress Juliana Berners – the very last word in snobs and
know-your-position-in-life addicts – states that only people of
certain ranks and stations should own particular hawks. According
to her *Duke of St Albans* (1486):

Eagle for an emperor
Gyr falcon for a king
Peregrine of the rock for the baron
Peregrine Tiercel [male] for the earl
Hobby for the squire
Merlin for the lady
Goshawk for the yeoman
Goshawk male for the poorman.

Well, poorman I was, so perhaps obtaining a female goshawk
put me just a little above my station, but what the heck! The
French nicknamed the goshawk *cuisinière*, or hunter for the kitchen, and this was all I wanted. I was scarcely interested in the
quicksilver acrobatics of the peregrine or merlin, and had decided
that any bird I kept must be no ornament, but would be required
to earn its keep. A goshawk would be exactly what I wanted if this

was the case. So I soaked up all the parlance, put together all the equipment I felt I needed, and even learned to tolerate fellow hawk-trainers and their ridiculous medieval garb. All I waited for now was the hawk.

The five weeks passed slowly, for I had a schoolboy's excitement about the arrival of my bird. I began to pester Eric the lecturer (what a carry-over from my Welsh childhood, Eric the lecturer, indeed) with phone calls that exhausted both his patience and my funds, but true to his word he arrived one Saturday morning with a tea-chest containing the hawk. I opened the chest in the eternal twilight of the darkened bedroom and my hawk flapped out. She was very similar to my buzzard in appearance, except that in place of Pelaw's puny claws, my hawk fielded scimitar-like talons. Above all, however, the facial expression was entirely different. Pelaw's eyes had been dark, trusting and friendly, but the goshawk's were a sort of paranoid yellow that reflected only the hatred she felt for mankind generally and me in particular, and I thought of Coleridge's Kubla Khan: 'Beware! Beware! His flashing eyes . . .' I stood looking at the bird fluttering in the stream of sunlight creeping in through the crack in my badly blacked-out windows. T. H. White has described the taming of a goshawk as a 'duel between man and bird with only God as umpire'. Time enough for duelling, however (and duel it was to be), for my eyass needed to be fully feathered before I took her up for training, and to grow those feathers she needed to eat. I would therefore feed her plenty and take her up for the duelling only when she was fully feathered.

It is possible to rear a goshawk almost entirely on raw beef, so the falconry books told me, but beef was expensive and it was a little hurtful to my pride to buy meat when I boasted of having some of the best hunting dogs in the country. I would hunt, therefore, to provide food for her. I would feed her whole carcasses which would yield all the vitamins her Finnish mother would have provided in her natural diet. So I set to straightening my rabbit snares, checked my rat traps and began the work. Fresh-killed rats – perhaps one a day – are ideal food for a hawk (providing one can be certain the rats have not been poisoned), for such a carcass will supply all the bone and much-needed fur to clean out the stomach. I caught a large buck rat the next day, bolted by my ferret and snapped up by my terrier. I tied the nasty scaly tail to a board so that my hawk might not develop the unpleasant habit of carrying off her prey, and walked up the stairs to the bedroom. She had heard me coming and was already frantically clawing at the window. 'Alarm the feeding hawk as little as possible,' I had been advised, so I placed the rat and board on the floor and slunk out, watching her through a hole I had drilled in the door (I am very destructive with property). She ignored my peace offering and went on fluttering at the window, so I shrugged my shoulders and left. Two hours later I returned and peeped through the hole. She was still fluttering at the window, but the rat was half-eaten – by morning it had disappeared.

The next few weeks were spent in daily hunting and scavenging to feed my ungrateful bird. I set snares for rabbits on the edge of the near-by game estate, put down break-back and catch-alive rat traps and took to scouring the country lanes for road casualties. Blackbirds, thrushes, sparrows – scarcely ideal food for hawks, so the falconry books told me – were frequent road casualties, and all graced my hawk's table, but ten days after her arrival my district experienced four days of heavy rain; so heavy, in fact, that the walls of the house became very wet and water poured into my kitchen. It was impossible to hunt and feed her. The danger of fasting a growing bird whose feathers still contained a liberal supply of blood was that her wing flights would develop fret work-like lines known as hunger traces, or lines of weakness, across which the feathers would snap in times of activity. On the fifth day, however, I set out to hunt again and before I reached the main road had found a half-grown leveret that had met its death through car, bike or, in mind of the last few days' rain, perhaps a passing ark. I raced back to the cottage and flung the carcass on the floor. All shyness and fear vanished in my hawk and she flapped to the floor to rip and tear at the carcass, her eyes still flashing with hate. The key to training was to be her belly. A hungry hawk is an obedient hawk, and a full-cropped bird is as wild as she was when first caught. Like Petruchio in *The Taming of the Shrew*, I would tame her by hunger, and also like Petruchio by waking her.

Next day, Eric, my mentor and hawk procurer, phoned to ask my progress and was astounded that I had not yet started on the training. His own tiercel, smaller but from the same nest, was already feeding on the fist. Smarting just a little at Eric's success, I phoned Denise and Stuart, two close friends who were used to my eccentric ways and who would not have been surprised if I had requested help with a rhinoceros. We set to to jess the furious hawk and fasten her to the screen perch. Next day I would begin training.

Medieval falconers broke a hawk by waking her, carrying her on their fists day and night until the bird fell asleep through sheer exhaustion. 'Stupid and pointless,' said Eric, but I had already resolved to compete in my duel with the bird and decided to wake her. I am a very poor loser at all indoor and outdoor games, for at the first opportunity I cheat! It is nearly impossible to beat me at any game, so skilful am I at cheating. (At one time I played solo chess, but cheated so often that I finished the evening hating myself.) So with cheating in mind I phoned Denise and Stuart and we resolved to take shifts carrying the bird, but first to get her to my fist. I unleashed her from her perch and held her by the jesses. She promptly went into one of the worst temper and fear tantrums I have ever seen, wildly flapping her wings and finally falling off my fist to hang upside down like a geriatric parrot in its last throes.

When we reached the sunlight she really went berserk, flailing the air and toppling from my fist as fast as I could put her back. But each time I gently lifted her back and waited for the next turn. So frequently did these tantrums occur that within an hour I developed a flick of the wrist that would put her back on the fist in a trice, but she continued to bate and beat the whole day through, glowering and panting after every temper turn and waiting only long enough to gain her breath before she erupted into another bout of frenzy. Morning faded into afternoon, and evening found the bird no better for my day spent with her. I was as exhausted as the bird, but every time I thought I had subdued her she went into another bate wilder than the last. Late that evening Stuart arrived with Denise, bringing food and prepared to take the night shift. T. H. White, in his glorious book *The Goshawk*, took three days and nights to subdue his bird, and Stuart and I steeled ourselves for the worst. I fell into a deep coma-like sleep, but at 3 a.m. was awakened by Stuart. The bird on his fist was sleeping soundly, so soundly that she allowed me to tuck her head under her wing and take all manner of liberties with her. Well, Katharina, like Petruchio I have waked you now to break you to obedience by hunger.

Next day I rose early and took the hawk on the fist. She erupted with the same exasperating fury displayed on the day previous, hanging limply by the jesses, turning like the pendulums of modern rotary clocks. I lifted her back to the fist, and again she exploded, frantic to be away from me. ('Told you waking was useless,' Eric said.) I tried to tempt her to eat a scrap of meat, grisly and nasty, with fragments of fur still adhering to it, but she disdained even to look at the horrid morsel. I drew it across her beak, and again she bated madly away from me. My patience was beginning to wear just a bit thin, and carrying her through the day did little to help, though towards the evening time, when the bustle of the day had diminished, her bates became just that much less furious. Evening found her still refusing the now rapidly browning piece of nastiness, however.

I almost relented and fed her in the sanctity and privacy of her darkened room, but was fortified by a phone call from Eric, stating that she must eat only on the fist or not at all. I therefore hardened my heart and she went to bed hungry. At dawn I took her up again, and again we went for our walk along the lanes, watched, I'm sad to say, by my badly neglected dogs. Again I tried to tempt her to eat, but she was steadfast in her refusal. The fourth day dawned, and with more than a hint of despair I fetched my screaming, bating bird. By now I felt decidedly foolish and frustrated. She had learnt so little and had taken up so much of my time. I was half-tempted to phone Eric and offer her back, when she displayed a decided interest in the sliver of meat I was dragging over her talons. By noon she was tearing shreds of meat and then, mistake of mistakes, I over-fed her. I stuffed her with a full seven ounces of meat and rabbit liver. Next day we returned to square one, for she was bating away from me furiously as I went to fetch her from her perch. I would not make that mistake again, but it put me back a full three days in her training. 'A hungry hawk is an obedient hawk.'

Three full days wasted, I reflected, and my gloom deepened when Eric's latest phone call informed me that his was coming to the fist on a full four feet of creance. I walked up the stairs and shouted a mass of foul, pointless obscenities at the mad bird, who toppled off her perch in unreasonable terror as I approached. 'Paranoid sod,' I hissed and left her to her antics. Time now to take my almost abandoned dogs for their run, but on return I was so exhausted I fell into a fitful sleep, punctuated by dreams of goshawks flying fast and furious after rabbits, striking down partridges and footing strange exotic birds unknown in Britain or anywhere else for that matter. The dawn alarm clock found me irritable and in an ugly mood. To anyone with an active mind, or anyone who likes to see results after hard work, the futility of carrying such a bird for days on end is maddening. Solitary walkers stared at me as I passed by them, trying to placate the terrified bird. Postmen smiled, then smiled more frightened smiles and turned their bikes to the far side of the lane to avoid us – a crazy bird perched on a lunatic.

She was not yet ready for the village and the hosts of horrid children who would swarm over to look at her, so our walks were around lonely lanes frequented only by farm hands and the hardier variety of courting couples. It was time for reverie and con-templation, and perhaps the most formative period of my life when I began to realize that when Thoreau, a forest dweller like myself, said, 'A man is rich in proportion to the number of things he can do without,' he could just about have been correct. I had so little in the way of personal wealth, but I had led an active, full life, untied and unbroken by the presence of wife and family, unrestricted by the hopes of promotion and uncluttered by the respectability required of most professional people. My belly was empty but rarely, and I was living exactly as I wished. Below me in the valley went cars and people, beetles and ants in the asphalt-jungle competition – a raptorial rat-race. Executives would shake their heads in disapproval at my hunting and then boast of making a 'killing in the city'. Let them scoff, ridicule and despise my way of life, I am a half-madman in an all-mad world and I would not change my lot with anyone.

Enough of thoughts and philosophy and back to training. A day's hunger did wonders for my bird, and the morrow found her eager to take food from my fist. Carry her all day, feed her little, keep her sharp set, ever eager for food, that would be my way, and I must not weaken my resolve. Three days of tiny morsels of rabbit meat, and she was stepping off her perch to be fed on a sliver of meat that would not have surfeited a blow-fly. Her weight was dropping steadily, and next day she jumped a full four inches to my fist. She jibbed at coming further, running up and down her perch, plaintively begging for the food but fearful of the flying jump necessary to make my fist. Remember your resolution, man – so I starved her another day and she came four feet to my glove, hitting it with a smack and eagerly looking for slivers of meat as a reward. Things were great, but whenever fate smiles on me I can expect a good kick in the backside immediately I turn around – and I got it.

Next day I walked the lanes again and tied my hawk to the gatepost to rest my hand and reflect happily on the progress made. Oh, cruel fate – a collie emerged from a near-by farm, barking and menacing. My hawk bated madly and her struggles were rewarded. She flew off over the top of the near-by copse, taking leash and jesses trailing after her. I searched for her for four long days, but she was gone. Pandora's box was wide open, and all the heartache and unhappiness imaginable rushed out. It was bad enough to lose a hawk, but to lose a hawk with a leash hanging from its legs – a leash certain to tangle in some branches and cause the bird to die a lingering death through starvation . . . Denise rang and asked if I wished to spend an evening with her and Stuart, but tactfully I declined – gloom such as mine was contagious and best kept isolated.

If only I had belled my hawk with those dross-ridden bells made by Mohammed Din, then at least her panic at being trapped and tangled would resound through the surrounding woods. Most hawks are belled by tying the bells by means of strips of leather called bewits to the legs, but goshawks, which kill with their massive talons, are belled by tying the bells at the base of the tail, leaving the talons free to foot the quarry while the tail, held at a jaunty angle, can ring out. 'Jessed but not belled,' Shakespeare had described one of his heroes – a quote that sprang so easily to mind as I contemplated the disaster.

Some five days later I was in the process of reading Edgar Mittel-holzer's *Kaywana Stock*, hoping that a little indiscriminate slave whipping would cheer me up. I can remember thinking that it is a brave author who will call his heroine Woglinde Prutt when my phone rang. I made a quick mental note that what I wanted for my birthday was an octoroon wench and picked up the receiver. A neighbour some miles from my house had trapped 'a bloody great thing with a dog lead hanging from its legs' in his garage. It had flown in, carrying with it a half-grown rat. I raced over to fetch her. Lady Luck had at last smiled on me – for the first time in months.

I arrived back at the cottage happy and contented, my misery now dispelled and quite undeterred at being back to square one in the training programme. A hawk gone feral for three days is as wild as when first caught – the thought passed through my head as I walked up the muddy lane, but time was the one thing of which I had plenty. I had made a shaky start at training, anyway, and a quick look at my mistakes, a second chance, so to speak, was all I required. She bated furiously all the way up the lane, but that was to be expected. A full crop of rat and five days of liberty was hardly conducive to producing an obedient hawk. Wake her again ('Useless, useless,' pleaded Eric), reduce her weight just a little and carry her often, and I would be back in training again before you could say 'Frederick II.' She had also learned to kill, for it was unlikely that she would have found the carcass of the rat, so she would be less trouble to enter, I reflected. Some falconers used to turn loose young hawks to learn to kill and fly at liberty, a period of freedom called 'hack' by falconers, so that they could develop strength of wing and learn to catch prey before being re-trapped for re-training. I would look on this period of freedom from her escape to recapture as a sort of period of hack. I was young in those days and hope sprang not only eternal, but also bubbled up madly until it overflowed the boundaries of reason.

So to begin again, and this we did by waking her and, by judicious deprivation of food, reducing her weight still further. Ten days later she was flying four feet to the fist again, and I noted with some malicious glee that Eric's tiercel's training had come to an abrupt halt for some reason or another. August loomed on the horizon and school broke up for the summer vacation. The last day at school began and I left the house, eager and itching to return and resume my training of the hawk. Last days of term are usually bedlam. In spite of the head's 'This is what will be done' morning briefing, the day is invariably disorganized and there is usually little to do. Satan is said to make work for idle hands (my mother's favourite cliché, always uttered as I sat down to read), and with 3 Removed (how curiously heads label troublesome classes) Satan would have had a field day. While I desperately tried to total up my most inaccurate registers, a scene resembling the Battle of Hastings was being enacted in front of me. Chalk and paper darts flew like arrows at Agincourt. Herod, who put a host of innocents to the sword, must have been a saintly old gentleman, I reflected cynically. School ended, and as I watched the avalanche of children crashing and rolling out of the gates, I was struck by how accurate the phrase 'school is breaking up' actually was.

Thus, with school over, I walked down the hill towards my cottage with three of my class, who chattered on about the forth-coming holidays, blissfully unaware that their first piece of work next term would be to write an essay entitled 'What I Did in the Holidays'. Oh God, we teachers are a boring lot, but I was un-heedful of the noise. My thoughts were now completely on Kate, as I now called my hawk, after Shakespeare's shrew. I raced up the hill towards my cottage, rapidly throwing off the tedium and weariness of the day and eager to resume battle with my adversary. Kate sat on her screen perch in her darkened room and, wonder of wonders, bated towards me as I opened the door. I fed her a tiny sliver of flesh to reward her for her enthusiasm, to whet her appetite, and then put her back.

Sitting downstairs drinking my tea, I felt very pleased with myself, musing, 'I was born to tame you, Kate,' and similar pointless egocentric quotes. So my first task was to go back upstairs for my hawk, to tie her to the front gate and then to back away and call her. She shuffled along the gate, hunched her back like Quasimodo contemplating another lunge at the bells and flapped seven feet to my fist. Another tiny sliver of flesh and back to the gate she went. I felt an elation hard to describe. Trainers of beasts, explorers, poets, may be able to understand, but no one else could. I walked away nine feet, and before I could turn she was flying to me to be fed. I picked her up. It was enough success for one day – and triumphs of this nature are heady draughts, inclined to make the trainer do something reckless. She was well behaved during a walk up the lane, bating only twice, once at the collie who had caused her first escape, and once towards a wood pigeon which flapped noisily off its perch in the elm trees. Woodies – what strange birds, hated, despised, persecuted, and yet still on the increase, ever eager to give away their presence by their noisy wing-beats.

I sat down back in my cottage feeling overjoyed. One last party to celebrate my victory over Kate – the forthcoming victory, that was, for I was younger then and still counted chickens before the eggs were laid, let alone hatched. I was at last well on the way to becoming a falconer. Celebrate! I walked to the village and bought two pints of sherry of a rare vintage – as much as I could carry away for 40p – and thought of Hogarth's Gin Street sign: 'Drunk for 1d, Dead Drunk for 2d.' Company! I phoned Denise and Stuart, but though I let the phone ring for ten minutes, there was no answer. Well, what the hell. I sat and drank the whole two pints in two and a half hours, and as I have an excellent head for alcohol – I became very drunk and very, very, sick.

Noon. I was still retching and vomiting, vowing never to touch any form of liquor again, shielding my eyes from the scantily clad women in the paper, enticingly advertising Cinzano – bright-eyed fillies who drank their weight and stayed coherent and happy in spite of it. Time to douse my unshaven face and half-crawl upstairs to see Kate. I had fed her only two ounces of rabbit the night previous and she was ravenous. I winced, the flapping of her wings and sounding like the rushing of winds in my alcohol-poisoned head. Down again to settle my turbulent inside with liberal amounts of tea, but it was 2.30 before I could stand properly, let alone resume battle. But pluck up courage I must, and she was very eager to be fed.

Ten, twelve, sixteen feet to the fist. How could she possibly fancy the ghastly, macerated rat I held in my fist, as I choked back my nausea and trying not to look at the cadaver? In spite of my heaving inside I resolved to walk her in the cool of the evening. There is something glorious about walking a hawk and a well-trained lurcher along country lanes. Jane, my lurcher, was disinterested in the hawk. She had seen all manner of creatures pass through my hands and all manner of lunacies manifest themselves in her master. We walked the lanes to the twittering alarm calls of blackbirds. They could never have seen a wild goshawk as they became extinct in the district three centuries ago, but the sight of those talons and that beak must have rekindled some unpleasant race memories.

The evening was cool and pleasant. A falconer walking his hawk seems to be moving in slow motion in a madly racing world. What a crazy life the average man leads from dawn till dusk, a slave of tradition, work and respectability. I crossed the road at the newly created pelican crossing, the sign of which read, somewhat ambiguously, 'Do not cross while the little man flashes,' and wandered to Denise and Stuart's house on the far side of the village. Let Kate see cows, dogs, horses and cats. Let her experience life as it really is – full of cars, caravans and crazy people. In four days' time I would fly her free of the restricting creance that had bound her to me this seven weeks or more, and chance her flying off.

Days passed, and she was coming forty feet as soon as I turned and called her. An experienced falconer would have flown her free after twenty feet, but I was not experienced and was reluctant to lose her again. I neglected to feed her on the day before she flew free, and she was famished when I took her up that lunchtime, nosing my fist for scraps of meat and looking as plaintively as only a hawk can look to be fed. This was the ultimate test, the penultimate anyway. After I took her up I looked almost longingly at the folded creance on the window ledge. I nearly repented and put it back on her, my conscience shrieking, 'You'll lose her. You'll lose her.' No, she must fly free today, and I was delighted that she seemed more than keen on the food I had in a plastic bag. (Falconers usually have elaborate bags made from embroidered and embossed leather with some lengthy inscription from Mitchell or Blaine stamped into it. I think mine said 'Mother's Pride' or something of the sort!)

To the gate we walked – my heart beating madly. I put her on the cross-members of the gate and walked away, fearing to look back lest it upset her and cause her to fly off, but I had scarcely gone six feet before she flew to my arm, clinging and flapping wildly. I fed her a morsel that served only to make her keener and walked away again. She flew thirty feet to my glove. After four days of savouring the pleasures of flying a free hawk, the magic began to cloy. Time now to find quarry for her to fly.

Goshawks are amazingly versatile and unselective about their quarry. Short of a goose or a heron (and I am told some goshawks will fly these), they will make a bid for most quarry. They will, when young and foolish, catch or at least try for hares, but in a very short time the kicking, bucking, rolling and general demeanour of a terrified hare convinces them that they would be better employed finding easier prey, and they will refuse to try for a hare even though they may be frantic to eat. Male goshawks are considerably smaller, and they feel the same way about rabbits as the female will about hares – they will try for them when young, but soon learn the error of their ways. Kate, I was determined, would be a rabbiting hawk, for I am of a plebeian nature and totally

119

unimpressed by the taste of aristocratic game. I am well content to sup on coneys and forgo well-hung partridge or pheasant. So it was to rabbit that I tried her first.

My four days of calling her to the fist had passed uneventfully. She had become quite obedient – for a goshawk, that is – and I was learning to regulate her weight. Too fat, by even an ounce, and she would go back to her wild bating and struggling as I approached. Too thin, and she would not be strong enough to hold her prey. Furthermore, a light hawk is prone to disease and illness. I learned in time to keep her at exactly the right weight, and the night previous to my attempt my joy was made all the more intense by a phone call from Eric telling how he and his tiercel were a good week behind me in training.

Time now, however, to put my kitchen hawk to the test. She was hungry, or 'sharp set', as they say in falconry circles, when I took her up at 6 a.m., and she gripped my fist in a vice-like grip that boded well for the day to come. I walked her for two hours through the fast-evaporating dew, fed her nothing, took her home and put her back on her perch. Jane, my rough-coated lurcher, watched my mounting excitement with interest. She had a strange perspicacity common only to mongrel dogs who are required to work for their living. Lurchers are peculiar dogs, bred as they are from a morass of breeds slightly ameliorated with greyhounds for speed. They also possess a sagacity unknown in other breeds tainted by the show bug. Jane knew my every mood, the excitement that preceded a hunt, the heavy tread and downcast expression which told that things had not gone well. That evening she was obviously baffled by my excitement, which must have been obvious even as I was eating my tea. At seven o'clock I took the wildly enthusiastic Kate (made keener by hunger) from her perch and sallied forth in search of prey. She was gripping my glove tightly and watched for every movement of my right hand, but she was not to be fed. We walked to the edge of the lane and she bated eagerly at a jay that shrieked its warning before fluttering into the trees. She was as ready as she would ever be.

I turned the corner and headed for Long Pastures, perhaps an hour's walk from my home. Before myxomatosis blighted our countryside, this had been an almost legendary place for rabbits and had even yielded an amazing bag to parties of tweed-clad shooting men out to slay a few creatures before returning to the metropolis. To poach with a hawk seemed almost a joke really, but I had no better place to enter her. Rabbits sat out feeding perhaps twenty feet from the hedge, encouraged but not too encouraged by the still of the evening. Kate saw them and I had difficulty in restraining her. My efforts of the last few months would be rewarded, I was sure. I picked out my victim, my prey, and stalked with a cat-like action, stopping stock still when it noticed me. It had that perky Lucy Attwood rabbit expression that prevents many sportsmen from shooting them, but I knew I must steel myself against sentiment of this kind. I came within twenty yards of the now alerted bunny, who had stopped feeding. No use restraining Kate any more. She bated towards it and I let her go. With a rustle of feathers and flicker of jesses, she was after him with a reptilian-like earnestness. He realized his predicament immediately and was off, bobbing and weaving for dear life. A few seconds later I found Kate staring in anger undiminished by reason down a hole into which the rabbit had disappeared. 'Kate, good try. A good try, Kate,' I murmured, just a little disappointed. The next flight was even less fruitful. I flung her off but she didn't even see the damned rabbit and swung back to the fist to be fed.

Approaching dusk found a somewhat disillusioned man with a bewildered hawk, after five flights a little in doubt as to whether she was capable of taking a rabbit. Then I saw him – a perfect sitter. He was way out from the hedge and feeding unconcerned. I approached him carefully, stopping and starting, and held Kate back to prevent premature flight. The rabbit had an almost non-chalant attitude and expression, and as I came to within thirty feet of him I realized that it was not my stealth or Deerslayer style of woodcraft which had allowed me to get so close. He was nearly blind. The myxoma swellings on his face had almost closed both eyes, and he viewed the prospect of life or death with the complete indifference symptomatic of myxomatosis. Still, a rabbit is a rabbit, I said to myself, and flung Kate off. She careered into him, bowling him over, and he responded by galvanizing himself into action. She struck at him again, and again he bowled her off, but she had changed his course. He was no longer running for the main warren that housed his associates (who were incidentally all wiped out by the bug a month later), but had turned towards a patch of bramble with Kate hanging on to him like a rider in the Calgary Stampede. He disappeared into the brambles while she, running

121

like a secretary bird, raced in after him. I ran after the combatants. She had him all right, but she was unable to finish him. I crawled in regardless of the thorns and killed him, dragging both rabbit and hawk from the brambles.

I had never been so jubilant – except perhaps when asked to leave a particularly unpleasant little school near Bromsgrove. My kitchen hawk had made her first kill. So, it was diseased, a poor substitute for the real McCoy – a creature half-dead anyway. What did that matter? I began to sing happily all the way up the lane, passing a courting couple who looked at each other in amazement. Success! The result of ten weeks' hard work. I fed Kate both the rabbit's hind legs and some liver and watched her crop distend and her defiance grow. She would go back, be bating and intractable for four or five days, but what the devil. I closed the door of the mews. Tonight excitement would banish sleep. Celebrate! I left the house and headed for that damnable off-licence and its sticky, poisonous sherry . . .

The August vacation passed rapidly and I hunted most days with her. I learned so many things during that warm, pleasant summer – to feed her to excess once a week with a nourishing meal of flesh, bone and fur that would help maintain her condition – but try as I might I failed to get her to take wrangle, the small stones that some falconers are so adept at getting into the gullets of hawks to clear out the slimy stomach waste. Her feathers were becoming very tatty, for when in yarak, a state of hunger keen enough to ensure the bird tries hard, she would crash into cover to kill any rabbit or moorhen that sought refuge there. Broken wing-feathers seriously hinder a hawk's flying ability, but this can be remedied by grafting or imping other wing feathers on to the stump of the feather still left in the flesh. Most falconers use hawk feathers saved from a previous moult, but I was unable to obtain them.

By late August, Kate had two feathers from a jay I had taken from a keeper's gibbet and imped into her wing. By October she resembled a science-fiction bird – a hybrid of jay, hawk and jackdaw. She looked remarkably scruffy, but her toll of quarry was truly formidable. Kate became deadly with rabbits and held them with great skill and dexterity. Goshawks will slay rabbits all day if allowed to. Many pre-myxomatosis falconers recorded twenty-four or so rabbits taken in one day by a large female goshawk. My tally was considerably less, I am glad to say, though Kate would have slain them till the cows came home. I hunted to eat and have always disliked wasteful butchering of game. Any survival-level hunter who takes massive hauls of rabbit instead of allowing a patch to keep most of its rabbits – treating it a bit like a walking larder – is a damned fool. I took three with Kate on one afternoon and fed two to the stock, but I was reluctant to bleed my hunting places white.

Rats are easy meat for a goshawk, and the fact that when bolted they skulk in the hedgerow (unsporting) presented no problem to Kate who, when in yarak (that word again), would crash into any hedgerow after one. She once nearly drowned as a result of an over-anxious bid at rats. We were hunting the edge of a small pool for young mallards when Kate began to bate frantically at something in the reeds. I thought at first that she could see a mallard or even a moorhen, and against my better judgement threw her off. She crashed into the reeds and a large buck rat ran squeaking out of the tangled vegetation. She took to the air again, but only a matter of five feet into the air mind you – goshawks rarely attain any height in the way a falcon does. The rat, of course, was far from happy with his lot, and took to the water, swimming like an otter and causing V-shaped ripples. Kate hit him and he vanished from sight and she was damned near drowned. I raced in to fetch her, and she allowed herself to be picked up spluttering and gasping. She still held the dead rat between her talons, preferring to drown rather than release it. She encountered a similar problem when she struck a moorhen above a pool and both crashed into the water. On that occasion the moorhen escaped.

In late September she encountered prey that bested her decisively, however. Jane and I were walking through the stubble of a newly cut cornfield and I was carrying Kate, mainly for the ride, so to speak. A hare was feeding on the clover able to flourish now that the corn had gone. Jane was after it in a trice, but I shouted her off when I saw the hare doubling back towards me. Kate lunged and I slipped her. To her it was a large rabbit, and she was more than able to foot a rabbit and hold it. She came down, tail braking, on the hare's muscular hind quarters. It rolled, kicked and threw her off with contemptuous ease and she landed winded on the grass near-by. Again she rose and again she footed him.

Again he rolled and again he kicked her off, and this time one of the kicks really went home. Anyone who reckons a hare to be easy quarry even for the strongest goshawk had best try holding a live one themselves. I was once frightfully lacerated and bruised when I tried to hold a live hare caught by the hind legs in a snare. Kate failed to hold her hare, a moderate-sized jack hare, not a huge doe, and came back to the fist, looking very forlorn and with several feathers missing. Many falconers state that they have hawks who take hare regularly. Mine failed, and God knows, Kate tried hard enough. Henceforth she would not even try once she had ascertained that the quarry sitting out in the field was a hare not a rabbit. Once one jumped up under my feet and Kate bated at it more in surprise than in earnest. I threw her off, and she circled the racing beast and put in a half-hearted putt, just for good measure, but then returned to the fist.

The easiest quarry for a hawk is certainly the moorhen, and even an indifferent hawk will fly these well enough. Somehow these quaint little water birds manage to survive and even to multiply – though how they do it I just don't know. They are sitting ducks (bad pun that) for any predator, be it dog fox or hawk, and any gunman short of a bit of sport will take his spleen out on these rather pathetic little creatures. I like moorhens and am reluctant to fly them. Furthermore, a hawk fed moorhen in its oilskin capsule soon goes off condition. I have eaten moorhen, but it is essential to skin rather than pluck them. The flesh is not unpleasant, though it is decidedly tasteless.

Towards the end of that winter I attended a falconry meet. It was a rather splendid affair, but in spite of this I took my tatty, imped bird along, perhaps to see if she had a chance to show off. I arrived and found magnificent hawks, and even more magnificent owners strutting about and proudly proclaiming the deeds of their birds – each one of the falconers talking in an anachronistic parlance that would have seemed a little artificial even at the time of the Crusades. One glanced at my ragged feather mop with her work-shattered plumage and pulled a face. 'Oh, no,' said one, 'in totally the wrong condition,' and proceeded to talk about his chanting gos and its exploits.

Shamefaced in the presence of experts, I put my bird back in the van and like a whipped cur followed at their heels. All had incredible stories of peregrines crabbing kestrels, of eagles taking an amazing number of foxes and of goshawks taking hare with contemptuous ease. I felt decidedly unhappy about my feats with Kate, relegated to her perch in the van. I listened and watched in awe and wonder as we approached the game area, but was astonished that when a rabbit 'got up' no one had a hawk in yarak to take it. Some had dropped a feather, some were not quite right, but no one had a bird that would fly. I felt very bitter at these 'experts' who had ridiculed my ragamuffin bird, her feathers damaged by hard work not by prancing about in front of a TV camera. Kate was a partner in hunting, a provider for the kitchen, while theirs had never had a feather ruffled during a hard struggle with a rabbit pulling them through gorse. I lost faith in most falconers that day. Falconers' tales are often so many feathery fishermen's stories.

What happened to Kate? Well, one day I flew her too heavy. It was a foolish thing to do. She was not in yarak and I should have known better, but she was becoming so tame that I started to take risks with her. She flew half-heartedly at an 'easy' rabbit and sat sulkily in a tree with one foot up, a sure sign of defiance – a sort of avian equivalent to a Harvey Smith gesture. I waited and called her. She totally ignored me – even yawning in her indifference and scratching her eye with her vicious talons. It began to rain, so I walked back to the house to fetch an anorak and a few pieces of meat to temp her to my fist. When I returned she was gone. I had kept her for seven short months which had passed magically but oh so quickly for me, and when she left she left an enormous gap in my life that was difficult to fill.

I wrote all over the world for another hawk, but was out of luck. Perhaps it was for the best. Kate would have been hard to replace. Some German falconer wrote to me offering goshawks in exchange for peregrines, but I had as much chance of trapping a peregrine as I had of catching a shooting star. Many falconers boast that they kept such and such a hawk for ten years and would scoff at my seven-month adventure, but it is easy to keep a hawk if one has no wish to fly it. I had had Kate for a little over half a year, and at least she had justified the soubriquet *cuisinière* – or kitchen hawk.

And so I shall end these tales of my adventures. I make no excuse for the life I have led and do not seek moral reasons for hunting. I hunt because I want to, for it is natural to me. Man is essentially a predator. He has the teeth for the job and the mental attitude to go with those teeth. Perhaps the meek will inherit the earth and the beatitudes are correct, but I fear there will be a devil of a lot of broken heads when they try to claim their inheritance.